Patric

Gagne

Memoir

Embracing The Sociopath Within

Maria F Giraldo

TABLE OF CONTENTS

PROLOGUE

My name is Patric Gagne, and I'm a psychopath. I am a passionate mother and wife. I am an engaging therapist. I am really charming and well-liked. I have many friends. I'm a member of the country club. I throw parties for every occasion imaginable. I reside in a lovely house. I'm a writer. I enjoy cooking. I vote. I make others chuckle. I have a dog and a cat, and I share carpool lines with other women who also have pets.

On the surface, I resemble nearly every other average American woman. Social media affirms my presence as a happy mother and loving partner, but my posts are borderline egotistical. Your friends would certainly describe me as pleasant. But, guess what?

I cannot stand your friends.

I am a liar. I'm a stealer. I am emotionally shallow. I am mainly resistant to remorse and guilt. I'm quite manipulative. I don't care what others think. I'm not interested in morals. I am not interested, period. Rules do not influence my decision-making. I am capable of virtually anything.

Sounds familiar?

If you picked up this book, I'm prepared to bet it will. You could be one of America's estimated fifteen million sociopaths. Alternatively, you could know one of the millions of people whose personalities are regarded to be on the psychopathic spectrum. And we're not just talking about criminals. Professionals include doctors, lawyers, teachers, and mail carriers. Sociopaths can be found almost anywhere. All you have to do is start looking.

The looking began early for me. While other children in my area were riding bikes and enjoying playdates with their friends, I was reading mysteries. Mostly true crime. I was fascinated by people's dark side. What makes them evil? What makes them capable? I wanted to know.

So when I came upon the term "sociopath," I assumed I had my explanation. I have heard the term before. But, what did it mean? What exactly constitutes a sociopath? I thought the dictionary would inform me. However, when I grabbed for my tattered, yellowing 1980 Funk & Wagnalls book, I realized that the term was missing.

Thinking it was a mistake, I went into my mother's office and opened another dictionary. Hers was an updated edition. "Sociopath" was sure to be present. But it wasn't. I noticed where it should have been—right between "sociology" and "sock"—but the word had vanished. It seemed as if it didn't exist. But I knew better. I'd read it in books. I'd seen it on the news. I had heard it in school. I'd written it in my journal. I knew the definition of "sociopath" existed someplace. I only needed to find it.

"Sociopath" is a mysterious term. Its origins can be traced back to centuries of science, but it has subsequently been hijacked to cover a wide range of sins. There is no single definition for the phrase now. The word, like the people it represents, has become rather paradoxical. A shape-shifting modifier whose meaning is frequently allocated through anger and indignation, "sociopath" elicits considerably more emotion than analysis. And why is that?

Why does the word "sociopath" elicit more emotion than thought? Ironically, I wanted to know this long before I was diagnosed. I made it my job to find out.

This book is the tale of that mission, which I felt compelled to write because the lived experience of sociopathy deserves to be documented. To be clear, I do not intend to downplay the severity of this condition. I don't want to romanticize it. Sociopathy is a dangerous mental disease whose symptoms, causes, and therapies require investigation and clinical attention. But this is exactly why I wanted to tell my story: so that people impacted by sociopathy can get the care they have been waiting for far too long. And, perhaps more importantly, other sociopaths may see themselves reflected in someone who has more to offer than evil.

Of course, not everyone can relate to my experience. I am only able to tell you this because of pure luck. It was fortunate that I was born into a world where I could enjoy practically every privilege possible. I am quite aware that if my ethnicity, class, or gender had been different, my life would have turned out very differently. Luck, in part, led me on a path to unraveling the riddle of my disease and creating a life in which I have been able to help others. Indeed, we are fortunate that this work exists at all. And it is fortunate that I have learned to appreciate the importance of relatability and representation.

Do you think you know a sociopath? I bet you're correct. But I'm willing to wager it's the last person you suspect. Contrary to popular assumption, sociopaths are more than only their personality traits. They are children wanting to comprehend. They're patients looking for validation. They're parents looking for solutions. They are humans in need of compassion. However, the system is failing them. Schools are not recognizing them. Professionals are not treating them. They literally have nowhere to turn for aid.

Representation is important. I'm sharing my experience because it highlights a truth that no one wants to admit: darkness lurks in the most unexpected places. I'm a criminal with no prior record. I'm a master at disguise. I've never been caught. I've rarely been sorry. I'm friendly. I am responsible. I'm invisible. I mix well. I am a 21st-century psychopath. And I wrote this book because I realize I am not alone.

CHAPTER 1

HONEST GIRL

When I ask my mother if she recalls the moment in second grade when I stabbed a child in the head with a pencil, her response is the same.

"Vaguely."

I believe her. Because so much of my early childhood is unclear. Some things I recall with complete clarity. Like the smell of the trees in Redwood National Park and our hillside home near downtown San Francisco. God, I adored that house. I still remember the forty-three steps from the ground floor to my fifth-floor room, as well as the chairs in the dining room that I used to climb to take gems from the chandelier. Other aspects are less obvious. Like the first time I snuck into my neighbor's house when they weren't there. Or where did I get the locket with the "L" engraved on it?

The locket contains two black-and-white images that I've never bothered to remove, and I can't stop glancing at them. Who were these individuals? Where have they come from? I only knew. I suppose I found the locket on the street, but it's much more likely that I stole it.

I started stealing before I could speak. At least, I believe I did. I don't remember the first time I stole something; all I know is that by the time I was six or seven, I had a whole box of stolen items in my closet.

A photo of Ringo Starr cradling me as a toddler can be found somewhere in the People magazine archives. We're standing in his lawn, not far from my birthplace in Los Angeles, where my father worked as a music producer, and I'm actually taking his spectacles. I certainly wasn't the first child to play with an adult's spectacles. But, based on the specs currently on my bookshelf, I'm quite sure I was the only one who stole a pair from a Beatle.

To be clear, I was not a kleptomaniac. A kleptomaniac is someone who has a constant and overpowering desire to take items that do not belong to them. I experienced a distinct form of drive, a compulsion caused by the discomfort of indifference, the practically inexplicable lack of ordinary social emotions such as shame and pity. But, of course, I didn't get any of this back then. All I knew was that I did not experience emotions in the same way that other children did. I didn't feel guilty about lying. When classmates were harmed on the playground, I felt no concern. For the most part, I did not feel anything. And I did not like how "nothing" felt. I took steps to create something from nothing.

It was early autumn, and I had just turned seven. I had been invited to a friend's slumber party, along with all of the other girls in my class. Collette lived a few blocks away from us. I arrived at her house wearing my favorite pink and yellow skirt. It was her birthday, so I insisted on carrying her present, a convertible Barbie vehicle wrapped in shimmering paper.

Mom gave me a hearty hug when she dropped me off. She was concerned about our first night apart. "Don't worry," she added, passing me my backpack and Holly Hobbie sleeping bag. "If you need to come home, you can."

But I wasn't concerned. In fact, I was thrilled. A full night in another location! I couldn't wait to start.

The celebration was enjoyable. We ate pizza, cake, and ice cream before changing into our pajamas. We threw a dance party in the living room and played yard games. But at nightfall, Collette's mother proclaimed that it was "quiet time." She started a movie in the living room, and we all arranged our sleeping bags in a circle. The girls fell asleep one by one.

When the film ended, I was the only one awake. There, in the dark, I became vividly conscious of my lack of emotion. I stared at my lifeless friends. It was disconcerting to see them with their eyes closed. I felt my stress rise in response to the emptiness, and I wanted to slap the girl next to me as hard as possible.

That's strange, I thought. I did not want to hurt her. At the same time, I was confident it would help me relax. I shook my head against the urge and inches out of my sleeping bag to get away from her. Then I got up and started walking around the house.

Collette had a baby brother, Jacob. His second-floor nursery had a balcony that overlooked the street. I carefully climbed the stairs and entered the room. He was sleeping, and I stared at him. He seemed little in his crib, much smaller than my younger sister. A blanket was balled up in the corner. I grabbed it up and adjusted it to fit his small frame. Then I focused my attention on the balcony doors.

As I unlocked the doors and went out into the darkness, the deadbolt clicked just slightly. From there, I could see the majority of the city. I stood on tiptoes and leaned forward to gaze up the street, focusing on the crossroads at the next block. I recognized the street name and realized it was one up from mine. I bet it would only take a few minutes to walk home.

Suddenly, I realized I didn't want to be there anymore. I didn't like being the only one awake, and I especially didn't like being so free. At home, Mom was always there to keep me in line. But here? Who would stop me? And what source? I felt uneasy.

It was dark as I walked out the front door, and I loved it. It made me feel invisible, and the strain I was feeling quickly dissipated. I got onto the pavement and began walking home, glancing at the houses as I went. What were the inhabitants like? What did they do? I hope I can find out. I wanted to be invisible and observe them all day.

As I walked home, the air was crisp and the streets were foggy. "Witching weather," my mother used to call it. At the crossroads, I removed my sleeping bag from my backpack and wrapped it over me like a giant scarf. The distance was greater than I had anticipated, but I didn't mind.

I looked across the street and saw a house with its garage door open. What's inside? I wondered. Then it occurred to me: I could go find out.

As I stepped off the curb, I was struck by how different the mood was. The rules, it appeared, had vanished along with the daylight. There were no limits in the dark, when everyone else was sleeping. I could accomplish anything. I can go anyplace. At Collette's place, the thought made me uncomfortable. However, the same potential had the opposite consequence. I felt powerful and in control. I was curious why there was a difference.

Moonlight lit my route as I approached the open garage. I stepped inside and had a look around. A beige station wagon was parked to one side, making way for an extensive collection of toys and knickknacks. Children must live here, I reasoned. My ankle bumped up against the deck of a skateboard. It felt like sandpaper.

Instead of taking it, I crossed to the car and opened the rear passenger door. A gentle glow from the dome light illuminated the garage, so I jumped inside and slammed the door behind me. I hesitated, waiting for anything to happen.

The silence inside the truck was terrible, but I preferred it. It reminded me of the Superman film and Christopher Reeve's visit to the Fortress of Solitude. "It's like my chamber," I said. I envisioned myself becoming stronger with every passing second.

Outside, a flash of movement drew my attention, and I noticed a car going past. My eyes furrowed as I watched the dark car pass. "What are you doing here?""I decided that the car was an adversary.

I quickly opened the door and tiptoed outside, just in time to see the sedan round the corner. General Zod, I thought defiantly. Then I dashed back across the street to where I had left my belongings. As I stooped down to retrieve them, I smelled the familiar perfume of laundry detergent and decided it was time to head home. I hugged the side of the sidewalk toward the trees. I picked up speed and found myself delightfully zigzagging between the shelter of the shadows. Why would anyone be terrified of the night? I pondered happily as I strolled. It's the highlight of any day.

I was fatigued by the time I reached the bottom of the hill leading to my house. I toiled up the steep incline, dragging my backpack behind me like a sled. The side door was open, allowing me to enter the house without knocking. I moved carefully up the stairs to my room, hoping not to wake my parents. My mother, however, barged through the door minutes after I had crawled into bed.

"PATRIC!"She yelled, slamming the light switch. "What are you doing here?!" Her reaction stunned me, and I started crying. In the hopes that she would understand, I recounted all I had done, but it just appeared to make matters worse. She started crying, too, her eyes wide with panic as tears streamed down her cheeks.

"Sweetheart," she eventually whispered, bringing me closer. "You should never, ever do something like that again. What if something happens? What if you were unable to come home?" I nodded in agreement, but neither of those issues bothered me. I was mostly perplexed. Mom had told me I could come home whenever I wanted. Why was she so upset?

"Because I said I would come get you," she explained. "Promise me you'll never do something like that again."

I promised, but I wouldn't get the chance to prove it for several years. Parents, I soon realized, usually frowned on playmates who came over for slumber parties only to become drowsy in the middle of the night and chose to walk home alone. Collette's mother was furious when she found out what I'd done, and she made no secret of it. After she informed the other parents about my disappearance, party invites stopped arriving. However, parents were not the only ones who were concerned. Other youngsters saw something strange about me.

Aside from my proclivity for thieving and disappearance, something about me made the other youngsters uncomfortable. I knew it. They were fully aware of this. And, while we could cohabit amicably as classmates, I was rarely involved in after-school activities. Not that I bothered; I enjoyed being alone. But after a while, my mother became anxious.

"I don't like that you spend so much time by yourself," she told me. It was Saturday afternoon, and she had come upstairs to check on me after several hours alone.

"It's okay, Mommy," I said. "I like it."

Mom frowned and sat on my bed, absentmindedly pulling a plush raccoon into her lap. "I just think it might be good for you to have some friends over." She took a break. "Would you like to introduce someone from school? How about Ava?"

I shrugged and gazed out the window. I was attempting to figure out how many bedsheets I needed to tie together to produce a rope long enough to reach the ground from my room on the top floor. Earlier in the week, I saw something called an "emergency ladder" in a Sears catalog and became obsessed with the notion of building my own. I wasn't sure what to do with it, but I knew I needed it. Only now, Mom was distracting me.

"I don't know," I replied. "I mean, Ava is nice. Maybe we should bring her over next month."

Mom threw the raccoon aside and stood. "Well, we're having the Goodmans over for dinner," she announced happily. "So tonight, I guess you'll just play with the girls."

The Goodmans resided on our block and were casual friends with my parents. Their two daughters were neighborhood terrors, and I despised them. Sydney was a bully, and Tina was an idiot. They were often in trouble, usually because of something Syd did, and I found their conduct irritating. Granted, I was in no position to pass judgment. But at the time, I justified my disgust. From my perspective, everything came down to intent. Whereas my behaviors were occasionally problematic, I wasn't breaking the rules for the sake of it; I acted out because I thought I had no other option. It was a form of self-preservation, preventing worse things from occurring. The Goodmans' acts, on the other hand, were irresponsible, attention-seeking, and malicious. They did awful things for no reason other than to be spiteful.

My sister, Harlowe, was four years younger and still a toddler. We shared the top floor of the house with our nanny, Lee, a lovely woman from El Salvador. Nanny Lee remained in the room next to ours. When the Goodmans came, she would usually be in Harlowe's room, putting her to bed. And rarely did a visit go by without Syd attempting to do something horrible to them.

"Let us sneak into Lee's room and dump water on her bed!" Syd hissed later that night, when we sat in my chamber.

I was already annoyed. "That's dumb," I said. "She'll know it was us, and then what? What are you getting out of it? She'll tell our parents, and you'll have to go home."

The barrette I had taken from Clancy was still attached to one of my strands. I began to tug on the clasp as I thought that the water dump might not be the worst idea after all.

Syd had cracked open the door and was looking outside. "Yeah, it's too late; she's already in her room. "She must have gotten Harlowe to sleep." She spun around. "Let us wake her up!Tina looked up from her magazine and snorted with delight. I was perplexed.

"Why?"

"Because then Lee would have to put her back to sleep!" And every time she does, we will wake her up repeatedly! It'll be really funny!"

It did not sound amusing to me. For starters, no one was teasing my sister. I didn't know how far it was between the fifth and fourth levels, but I was ready to "accidentally" shove Syd and her sister down the stairs if necessary. As for Nanny Lee, I didn't want her to come out of her room. I knew that the moment my sister fell asleep, Lee would phone her family and talk for hours. That meant I could listen to my Blondie albums uninterrupted.

At the time, I had acquired a fascination with Debbie Harry. I was obsessed with anything Blondie, particularly Parallel Lines. Debbie Harry appears on the album cover wearing a white dress, hands on her hips, and an angry expression on her face. I admired this photograph and wanted to look like her. So much so that if you look through my mother's photo albums, you'll discover more than a year's worth of photos in which I plainly try to recreate this iconic position.

Debbie Harry didn't smile on her record cover, so I vowed not to either—for anything. Unfortunately, after a catastrophic episode with the school photographer in which I kicked over a tripod, Mom decided that Debbie Harry was a "bad influence" and threw away all of my Blondie albums. Nanny Lee hadn't realized I'd taken them out of the rubbish and listened to them all night.

I decided to change tactics. "How about this," I suggested. "Let's sneak into the backyard and spy on our parents through the windows."

I could see Syd was irritated. My plan was somewhat ineffective because it did not entail torturing anyone. Nonetheless, the prospect of listening in on our parents' conversations was too appealing for her to pass up. Tina, too, appeared thrilled.

Syd agreed after some negotiations. We sneaked out of my bedroom and made our way past Nanny Lee's chamber in a single file. We eventually made it all the way down to the laundry room. I unlocked the door leading to the side of the home. California's air was both cool and sweet.

"Okay," I said. "You two go this way, and I'll meet you on the back deck." They were nervous. The yard was not only pitch-black, but also virtually nonexistent, as the majority of the home was supported by wooden stilts that fell a hundred feet down a hill. One errant step would send them tumbling to the ground. "You're not afraid, right?"I put on my most concerned expression.

Tina was the first to answer. "Get me a Coke," she urged before disappearing along the side of the house, Syd following reluctantly.

As soon as they were out of sight, I returned inside and locked the door. Then I crept upstairs to my room, turned off the lights, climbed into bed, and started my record player. I was peaceful and satisfied with myself. I knew I should have felt guilty about what I did, but I didn't. I was able to listen to Blondie uninterrupted.

It took nearly an hour before I saw my mother's shadow on the stairs. I flung my headphones on the floor and managed to turn down the noise just before she stepped through the door. "Patric," she inquired, "did you lock Syd and Tina out?""

"Yeah," I answered honestly. I could tell Mom didn't know what to say next.

"Well, the Goodmans are extremely upset," she continued, sitting on the bed next to me. "They got lost in the darkness and didn't know how to get back inside. They could have been hurt, honey." She hesitated and continued, "I doubt they'll ever come over again."

"Great!" I replied, ecstatic. "Tina always takes a bath in my tub with the lights turned off, which is ridiculous, and Syd always sneaks food upstairs and pours it all over the place. They're both quite obnoxious!My mother shook her head and moaned.

"Well, thank you for telling me the truth, sweetheart." She kissed the top of my head. "But you are grounded. "No going outside and no television for a week." I nodded calmly, accepting my fate. That was a tiny price to pay.

Mom stood up and made it to the stairs before I cried out, "Mommy?"She turned around and returned to my room.

I took a deep breath. "I got the Blondie records out of the trash after you threw them away, and I listen to them every night even though I know I'm not supposed to." Mom remained still, her gorgeous silhouette highlighted by the hall lights.

"Do you have them here? In your room?"

I nodded. Mom proceeded to my record player, where Parallel Lines was still playing quietly. She stared at me and shook her head. Then, one by one, she took the records and tucked them under her arm before kissing me one more. She moved the hair out of my face and across my brow.

"Thank you for telling me, my honest girl," she said. "Now good night."

Mom stepped out of my room and down the stairs while I rolled over and snuggled into my pillows. I brushed my feet together beneath the blankets, like a cricket. I felt safe and pleased. The record player continued to play, and the repetitive sound was relaxing. I watched the empty turntable spin round and round, and for a split second, I considered the wisdom of disclosing my secret and losing my Blondie recordings. Nonetheless, I smiled as I fell asleep.

CHAPTER 2

LAYERS

Things remained this way for a time. Dad rarely returned home before midnight, and my interactions with him were limited to quick kisses in the car before school and weekend activities. Not that I really cared. In fact, I enjoyed having my mother and sister all to myself.

I enjoyed having a sibling, period. I've heard that parents are concerned about jealousy and sibling rivalry, but these were never an issue for us. I didn't appreciate being the center of attention. When my sister arrived, I had someone to help me focus. And I enjoyed having a friend who understood my tendency for mischief. One-sided rule-breaking has always been at the forefront of our interactions, and it still is now. Harlowe would bring me a cup, which I would toss down the center of the stairway. Harlowe would step into the tub and point to the bubble bath, and I would empty the bottle and activate the Jacuzzi jets. Every action resulted in a frantic reaction. Mom adored it. However, the frantic sound of Harlowe's laughing did not always resonate with my father.

"What are you guys doing?" he inquired one day as he unexpectedly entered my room. He used to enjoy playing with us, but lately he seemed to only want to sleep while he was at home, which wasn't often.

Dad began to spend more and more time at work, and my mother eventually got despondent. Some days, she'd cry over the smallest of things. Other times, she'd get upset and snap at us for reasons I couldn't comprehend. I was frightened and bewildered, and for the first time, I couldn't rely on my mother for advice. She hadn't prepared one of her cakes in weeks, and there didn't appear to be a decent time to talk to her about what I'd been doing. Like stealing.

I had been taking backpacks from school. I didn't want them and almost always returned them. It was more like a compulsion, something I performed to relieve stress. When I saw an unattended backpack, I grabbed it. It didn't matter where it was or who had it; what mattered was that it was taken. Doing something I knew wasn't "right" was how I relieved stress and jolted myself out of my indifference. However, it eventually ceased working. Regardless of how many bags I took, I couldn't get that rush. I didn't feel anything. And I'd seen that the nothingness increased my desire to do horrible things.

It seemed a lot like the last time I saw Syd. We were standing on the sidewalk, ready to go to school, when she started getting on my nerves. She had wanted to stay the night at our place, but she was not allowed.

"It's all your fault," she complained. "If you hadn't pulled that silly prank on us, we could still come over and play with your toys. You always ruin things."

I said "sorry," even though I wasn't. I was relieved she wasn't permitted to visit. My head hurts. The pressure had progressively increased, and nothing I did seemed to help. I was emotionally distant, worried, and disoriented. It seemed like I was losing my mind, and all I wanted was to be alone.

Syd suddenly kicked my rucksack from where it was sitting at my feet, knocking everything to the ground. "You know what?" she asked. "I do not care. Your house stinks, and so do you."

The outburst was useless; she'd done it countless times before to garner my attention. But she had chosen the wrong day to start a quarrel. Looking at Syd, I realized I didn't want to see her again. I believed this message should have been obvious after locking her outside my house in the middle of the night. But I clearly needed to deliver a more direct message.

Without saying anything, I leaned down to retrieve my belongings. We had pencil boxes back then. Mine was pink with Hello Kitty figures and filled with sharpened yellow #2s. I grabbed one, rose up, and pushed it into the side of her head.

The pencil fractured, and half of it became lodged in her neck. Syd began screaming, and the other kids understandably lost control. Meanwhile, I was dazed. The pressure was gone. But, unlike any other time I'd done something wrong, my physical attack on Syd had resulted in something unexpected, a sense of exhilaration.

I walked away from the situation feeling perfectly at ease. For weeks, I'd been indulging in various forms of subversive conduct to alleviate the pressure, but nothing had worked. But with that one violent deed, all traces of pressure were removed. Not simply gone, but replaced by a profound sense of tranquility. It was as if I had discovered a shortcut to peace, one that was equal parts efficacy and craziness. None of it made sense, but I didn't mind. I strolled around in a daze for a while. Then I returned home and quietly told my mother what had happened.

"WHAT THE HELL WAS GOING THROUGH YOUR MIND?" my father asked. Later that night, I sat at the foot of my bed. Both of my parents stood before me, demanding answers. But I did not have any.

"Nothing," I replied. "I do not know. "I just did it."

"And you're not sorry?" Dad was furious and irritated. He had recently returned from another work trip, and they were fighting.

"Yes! "I said I was sorry!" I exclaimed. I had already written Syd an apology letter. "So why is everyone still so mad?"

"Because you're not sorry," Mom replied quietly. "Not really." "Not in your heart." She then stared at me as if I were a stranger. That look immobilized me. I recognized the expression on Ava's face from the day we played house. It was a foggy recognition, as if to suggest, "There's something strange about you." I can't exactly put my finger on it, but I can sense it."

My gut lurched, like if I had been punched. I despised the way my mother stared at me that night. She'd never done this before, and I wanted her to stop. Seeing her stare at me in that way seemed like being studied by someone who didn't know me at all. I became furious with myself for telling the truth. It had not made anyone "understand." If anything, it had puzzled everyone, even myself. I rose up, eager to make things right, and attempted to hug her, but she raised her hand to stop me.

"No," she replied. "No." She gave me another long, piercing stare before leaving. I watched as Dad followed her out of my room, their figures shrinking as they descended the stairs. I got into bed, wishing I had someone to hurt so I could experience the same emotions I felt after stabbing Syd. I settled for myself and pressed a pillow against my breast, driving my claws into my forearm.

"Be sorry!" I hissed. I continued to claw at my skin and clench my jaw, wishing for remorse with all my strength. I can't remember how long I tried, but I was desperate and enraged when I eventually gave up. Exhausted, I fell back into bed. I looked at my arm. It was bleeding.

Following the Syd incident, Mom distanced herself from everyone. For weeks, she rarely left her room, and when she did, she always appeared melancholy. Nanny Lee was basically in charge back then. I adored Nanny Lee. She was sweet and loving, and she always read books to us after we should have been sleeping. But all I truly needed was my mother.

The thrill I had experienced after stabbing Syd was both disturbing and alluring. I wanted to go through it again. I wanted to hurt again. Only, I didn't want to. I was confused and terrified, and I needed my mother to help me. I didn't understand how things had gone so badly. I just knew it was all my responsibility, and I needed to find a way to set things right.

I was upstairs in my room thinking about this one day when I detected a whiff of something familiar.

Chocolate cake.

She must have just gotten the layers out of the oven. That meant she'd put them in the freezer to cool before moving them to the dining room for slicing and frosting. And at that instance, I knew exactly what to do.

The box in my closet had once again become filled. Books, candies from the grocery store, LPs from my father's office, coffee mugs from the teachers' lounge, a pair of shoes—all of which I had lifted to relieve stress. I removed the box from its hiding location and placed it on top of my dresser. This. This was how I would make it up to my mother.

If she was baking cakes again, she must have been feeling better. I'd tell her about everything I'd done, and she'd help me make things right. She'd wrap me in a great hug and call me her honest girl. My mental box would be empty, and I'd have a clear slate to work with. The strain, the doubt, the tension, and the urge to harm would all go away the moment I confessed. I'd sit on the floor next to the table and practice my apologetic speeches while she finished the cakes, but this time I'd really mean it. She would be extremely proud of me.

I walked down the stairs silently, carrying the box behind me. It took some effort, but I eventually got it to the bottom floor, where I could look into the dining area without being noticed. The smell of chocolate pastries was rich and sweet, much like my mother.

I tightened my hold on the box as I leaned over the corner. I already had a mental image of what I would see: Mom in her peach dress and flats finishing the icing around the first layer of cake. I was so sure of this image that I gasped when I saw her sitting at the table, silently sobbing. All the lights were turned off. Her hands shook and the thread was limp as she attempted to cut through a layer of cake. The table was cluttered with leftover slices, each cut improperly and flung to the side. How long had she sat there? I will never know.

Her face was blotchy, and her apron was soaked with tears. She was hyperventilating, her head twitching slightly with each rapid breath. I jumped behind the corner and stopped, unsure what to do next. I had never seen her like this before. Her despair seems to consume her. From the living room, I could hear a strangled cry as another layer of cake crumbled. Then I heard the door open and realized she had left the dining room. I looked down at my box and realized it needed to go.

The sound of a mixer rang out from the kitchen as Mom proceeded to bake another cake. I bent down and carefully took up the package. Then I walked back up the stairs to my room, pausing at the landing of my parents' bedroom. I opened the double doors and headed to the wooden trunk at the foot of their bed. I knew this was my mother's hiding place. Parallel Lines was hidden inside a blanket and took me only a few seconds to find. I shoved the record under my arm and walked upstairs to my room, softly kicking the door open with my foot. When I turned on my record player, I didn't bother to put on headphones. Mom was too preoccupied to notice what I was doing.

The sound of Debbie Harry filled my room as I slid the box back into the closet. Two days later, I disposed of it by putting the contents into a rubbish can in front of Syd's home. Then I walked home without any sorrow.

CHAPTER 3

FLORIDA

"Pack a bag," Mom urged immediately after the stabbing occurred. "We're going to visit Grandma for the weekend." This is how my mother informed us that she was leaving my father and transferring us to Florida. I packed for the weekend without knowing any better.

Things in Florida were strange from the beginning. For one thing, my mother refused to confess that she had abandoned my father and that we had moved to Florida permanently. This remained true even after Dad had mailed the automobile (together with the rest of her belongings) so she could begin looking for a new home. Mom, I discovered, did not always tell the truth. And it was frustrating. I might as well just lie, I reasoned several times, because I'm going to be in trouble anyhow.

After a while, Mom seemed to realize that her choice to extend our family's vacation" was not settling well with my sister and me. To make up for some of her remorse, she eased a few of her strict restrictions. She even let me keep my first pet, a ferret named Baby. I adored Baby. Other than my sister, she was my sole true companion—and a formidable one at that. Baby was a lively rogue with a charming personality and a fondness for sparkly items. She was a natural born thief. Indeed, she would frequently roam my grandmother's house at night in quest of jewelry—earrings, necklaces, everything she could get her hands on—before dragging it back to the tiny bedroom I shared with my sister and adding it to the treasure trove she kept beneath my bed.

Every morning felt like Christmas. I'd wake up and drop to the floor to see what my four-legged Santa had delivered. I retained the things I liked for me. I left the things I didn't want alone.

"Good girl, Baby!" I commented one morning while holding out a dangling gold earring.

I kissed the ferret and then buried my nose in her neck, inhaling deeply. I'd heard that ferrets were unpopular pets due to their stink, but I adored the way Baby smelled. Her earthy aroma reminded me of books from the public library. Baby gnawed on my hair, signifying that she wanted to play.

I stood there, affixed the earring, and looked in the mirror. I then grabbed up the ferret and placed her in my knapsack. Baby sprawled out in a lengthy stretch. "Are you ready?" I questioned her. "Let's go!"

One advantage of living in Florida was the usual absence of surveillance. My grandmother was primarily in charge back then, and she was very liberal about children's independence. As long as my sister and I checked in on a regular basis and pledged not to travel more than two blocks from the house, we were virtually left to our own devices.

As the "weekend" at my grandmother's extended into months, I reverted to old methods of dealing with my internal stress. I stole money from the collection trays at church. I tossed roadkill in the yard of a nasty lady who lived down the street. I broke into a deserted house a few blocks away and spent my free time there, relishing in the silence.

I enjoyed it in the house. When I stepped inside, I felt instantly at ease. The blankness of the room mirrored how I felt, and I enjoyed the balance. I also enjoyed how, although being empty, the house felt filled. I could sit alone for hours in such frenzied silence. The absence of sensation, which usually worried me out, had the opposite impact in the empty house. In some strange manner, it reminded me of the Gravitron. The perennial county fair classic is a spinning ride with no seat belts or seats. Riders are pinned to the wall by centrifugal force. I used to enjoy it. Over and over, I'd spin, perplexed by the machine's operator, who sat in a control station in the center of the wheel.

I once questioned my mother, "Why doesn't he get dizzy?"

"Because he's in the exact center," she explained. "He's not affected by the spinning."

That's how I felt when I got to the house. Intellectually, I realized I was breaching some adult code, and that awareness put me in control of the trip. The home was pulsing all around me, horrified that it had been invaded, but I was calm in the center, at peace and in charge. I'd let Baby out of her rucksack and let her explore, then sit in the sunroom reading my books. It was blissful.

Of course, I understood I wasn't supposed to go into other people's houses and that I needed to tell my mother. After all, I wanted to be honest. I wanted to stay protected. But whenever I tried to confess, she appeared upset. There was never a good time to speak with Mom in Florida. She appeared to be avoiding me lately. She refused to address anything potentially upsetting. And I mean obvious stuff, like the fact that we were no longer living with Dad in San Francisco and had no plans to return. Even after she eventually found us a place to live—a little townhouse near the beach—Mom hesitated to reveal any details about her long-term ambitions.

"Mom, why are we going to a new school?" I inquired, as she drove her car through a carpool queue of strangers a few months after we moved into the townhouse.

"I don't know," she replied. "I just figured it might be more fun than sitting at home all day while Dad and I try to figure things out."

"Well, who's gonna take care of Baby?" I said, already missing my pet. "She's going to be so bored without me."

"I'll make sure she gets lots of attention while you're gone," my mother said. "In the meantime, maybe you could make some new friends."

"New friends?" I asked. "I didn't have any old friends."

"Well," Mom said hopefully. "Maybe this time will be better."

But it wasn't. The school could have been new, but I remained the same. The other kids were pleasant enough, but I could tell they noticed I was different. Granted, my behavioral "tells" were not particularly subtle.

"Have you ever French-kissed?" a kid named Ryan inquired. We were eating lunch in the cafeteria about a month after Mom had registered us in our new school.

"No," I replied.

"Why not?" Ryan pressed.

I laughed as soon as I said, "Because my mom died." The response didn't make any sense. I don't remember why I said that, but I was confident it would conclude the conversation. And it did, along with any hope of going under the radar. Ryan's expression, like those of the other children at the table, altered immediately. They all gave me the same look. I have seen it before.

The principal quickly learned of my mother's death and summoned me to her office.

"Patric," she remarked, sitting too close to me on her sofa. "I've heard your mother passed away. Is that correct, honey? Her expression was filled with concern.

"No," I replied, hoping to put her at ease. "She's not dead."

"Oh," she said, furrowing her brow. "Well, why did you say she was dead?"

I did not have an answer. It was a dumb lie, and it was extremely unusual of me. I knew it was a mistake, and I was also aware that it would almost certainly attract unwanted attention. I did it anyway. I wouldn't say I wasn't concerned about the consequences; I simply knew they wouldn't affect me. Even then, I knew there was a difference.

"Well, we were all talking about the worst thing that could ever happen," I'd said. "So that is what I said. My mother's death would be the worst thing."

The principal nodded earnestly and managed a grin. "That makes more sense," she replied. "You and your sister seem like such sweet girls."

She was half correct. Harlowe was a nice girl. My sister was already doing well in school after only a few weeks. She'd been on countless playdates and was undoubtedly the most popular girl in her class. People were instinctively drawn to Harlowe. She was like Dorothy from The Wizard of Oz, making new friends wherever she went. But I was like a blond, ferret-toting Wednesday Addams, casually repelling everyone in my path.

I occasionally attempted to blend in—to act "normal" like the other kids around me—but it never worked. For starters, my exposure to traditional conduct and reactions was confined to my immediate family, so I could only pretend for so long. But, more significantly, I didn't have somebody to instruct me. My difficulties to conform felt similar to those of a student in my class who struggled with reading. He excelled at math and music, but he had a learning handicap that made it difficult for him to read letters. He'd been assigned a specific instructor who helped him improve his skills.

Perhaps that is what I have, I reasoned one day. A sense of incapacity.

I wondered if the men within the prison had had a similar experience. It seemed as if everyone else intuitively understood the complete range of feelings. Some emotions came effortlessly to me, such as rage and enjoyment. However, some emotions proved more difficult. Empathy, guilt, embarrassment, and jealousy were like languages I couldn't speak or comprehend.

Is there a special instructor who can assist me? I knew that pupils who needed extra assistance were expected to go to their teacher. But I couldn't do it. Mrs. Ravenel, my fifth-grade teacher, was the meanest in school. So much so that disobedient pupils were sent to her rather than the principal for punishment. She had no tolerance for children who were different.

"Well, what do you want?" She once questioned a Black second-grader who had been sent to our classroom for talking too loudly. "Do you want me to take you outside and hang you from a tree by your thumbs?" "Is that what you want?"

The tiny boy began shaking and crying. All the other students in class were laughing, but I was furious.

Hanged from a tree? I thought. For talking? Even though Mrs. Ravenel informed us that youngsters "like that" needed to be taught a lesson, I didn't understand. I may not have felt an emotional connection to the concepts of good and wrong, but I was aware of their existence. What this teacher was doing was incorrect. She was emotionally abusing a child. Worse, she enjoyed it.

It's better to be like me, I reasoned.

It was the first time I understood that fear could not be used against me. It wasn't that I was impervious to it; rather, my response was subdued. I knew this wasn't the situation for most children. My students were terrified of Mrs. Ravenel, but I was never scared by her antics. My relatives were terrified to leave the house after dark, but I had no issue walking around the neighborhood alone. And while my sister was calmly playing in our room after school, I was breaking into neighboring houses. Could I have been caught? Sure. Was I concerned about the consequences? No. I had decided that fear was a meaningless emotion. I felt sorry for folks who appeared to be terrified of everything. What a waste! I was pleased to follow my own rules and live freely. Apprehension served no use for me.

But everything changed when I met the man and the kitties.

"I just found them," he said. "Would you like one?"

My sister and I were playing outside in the late afternoon after school. Mom had decided to earn her real estate license and was gone a lot during those days, which didn't quite fit with her "we aren't here permanently" narrative. Several days a week, Mother would send me and Harlowe to my grandmother's house after school so she could study. We usually spend our exile on the back patio, but that day we opted to pick flowers in the front yard. We could grab as many as we wanted while no one was looking, including buds from my grandmother's rose bushes that we weren't permitted to touch.

"What color are they?" I asked him.

"Well, what color do you like?" He appeared genuinely pleasant.

"Black," I declared decisively. I had always wanted a black cat. Baby would too! I envisioned the three of us having a great time inside the vacant house, my ferret and cat playing joyfully in the yard as I sat in the sunroom watching.

The man asked Harlowe, "And what color do you like?" She grabbed my hand and gently pulled me back toward the house, refusing to look at him.

"Oh, you don't have to be afraid of me, sweetheart!" he said to her. "Besides," he added, returning his gaze to me. "I just happen to have two black kitties. One for each of you. They're right around the corner. Want to come have a look?"

"Sure!" I spoke without hesitation. But Harlowe wouldn't have it. She tightened her grip on my hand and began walking backwards.

"No," she replied gently.

No? Was she crazy? This man was providing two black kittens for free, and she wasn't going to accept it? I understood why. She was afraid. But that was not my problem. I released my fingers from her vise grip and kissed her on the forehead. "I'll be right back."

"No!" Harlowe spoke again. Except that I was not listening. I followed the man down the street and toward the crossroads.

"They're just over here to the left," he told me.

As I came around the corner, I glanced at my sister. She stood in the middle of the street, terrified. Why is she afraid? I wondered. The question nagged me.

I turned back to look at Harlowe but couldn't see her anymore. We were now on a different street, the one with the house where I used to hide. I observed a van parked in the driveway. The man motioned for me to follow him as he proceeded toward it.

"That's my van there," he said, "in front of our house."

That's when something clicked. I knew no one lived in the house. It was my vacant house. He was lying, and I had made a horrible mistake. I was in danger.

The van door was open, and a woman sat in the back, next to a cardboard box. "Come look!" she beckoned to me. "They're so cute!" But I didn't have to take any further steps to realize there were no kittens within the box. What I needed to do was make sure this pair didn't realize I was on to them.

It was too late to run. The man had walked back alongside me, obstructing any escape to the roadway. I instinctively leaned into my lack of feeling. I turned to him, seeming to be friendly, and smiled brightly.

"Is that your wife?" I inquired. "That's really sweet! "She's keeping the kittens company so they're not lonely!" The man cocked his head, unsure what to think. I waved to her and asked him, "What's her name?"

His instinct was warning him not to trust me. I could see it on his face. He was giving me a look. Despite his instincts, he smiled again and moved away from me. "Anna," he asked, "will you scoot over so our new friend can get a look at those kittens?"

But I had already gone. I began to flee the moment the man turned his head, the angry sound of his voice as he roared after me casting doubt on his genuine intentions.

Fear, I discovered that day, may be useful.

CHAPTER 4

ALERT

"Baby died."

I was in the living room, watching television, when Mom told me. It was several months after our visit to the prison. Harlowe had discovered our pet cold and lifeless on the floor, and my younger sister was wailing in the upstairs bathroom.

"Patric, did you hear me?" Mom inquired, irritated.

I had, but I didn't know what to do about it. The news of Baby's death was a shock that would not go away. It was bouncing about in my mind. I blinked a few times, nodded to my mother, and resumed watching television.

She went upstairs to console Harlowe after expressing her displeasure with a heavy sigh. And, for the first time in memory, I was envious. I wanted to weep upstairs, too. I hoped I could be in the toilet, lying on the floor and sobbing alongside my sister as waves of genuine anguish crashed over them. I knew I was "supposed" to be just as clearly sad as my sister. So, why wasn't I?

I checked my reflection in the sliding glass door. I closed my eyes and focused until I felt tears fill up beneath my lids. I looked again. That was more like it, I thought.

The girl behind the glass, tears running down her cheeks, appeared to have recently lost a pet. She looked like she needed comforting. But I knew the female on my side of the glass couldn't look that way unless she made an effort. I blinked, and my attention lapsed. The tears vanished. I resumed my focus on television.

To claim I felt nothing is not accurate. I adored Baby more than anything else in the world. I couldn't believe she was no longer alive. But here we were, and she wasn't. When attempting to convey this lack of certain emotions, I've compared it to standing next to a roller coaster. I can hear everyone on the ride. I can see the track's dips and turns. I can feel the rush of adrenaline as the train begins its steep rise. As the first car approaches the top of the hill, I draw breath into my lungs before exhaling hard with my palms over my head, watching the coaster rush to the bottom. I got it. I'm just not experiencing it firsthand.

I could tell my mother had no idea what to do with a kid like me. She expected a normal child with normal reactions, just as any reasonable parent would. The fact that I couldn't offer her what she wanted caused me to experience what I called "stuck stress." It, too, reminded me of a roller coaster, but not in the way I experienced it. Rather, it was the sensation just before launch, when the over-the-shoulder harnesses would fall into position. For everyone else, these restrictions symbolized safety. Security. But not for me. I despised the way they entrapped me. I couldn't conceal it if I needed to. Unable to breathe. The claustrophobia developed whenever I realized I wasn't experiencing what others expected me to feel.

That is how I was the night Baby died. I could hear my sister crying. I could envision the waves of sadness. It's simply that I wasn't standing in the ocean among them. It wasn't so much that I lacked the feeling as that I felt disconnected from it, like my reflection in the door. I could see my feelings, but I was not attached to them.

I turned the TV off. I may not have been able to communicate (or experience) my emotions in the same way that I imagined others did, but I understood that nonchalantly watching reruns of Dallas while my first pet lay dead in the next room would only lead to issues. I proceeded to the laundry room, where I assumed Baby's body lay still. Maybe seeing her for myself would make me feel more…what? I did not know. Mom had wrapped the ferret in a holiday-themed dish towel, and bright Christmas trees surrounded Baby's small body.

She must have been freezing, I thought. She sat near the dryer to get warm. I bent down and cautiously lifted the cloth. Baby remained underneath, her eyes partially open. I hung my head and breathed, thinking, "This sucks."

I gazed at Baby again and noticed that she appeared both completely familiar and foreign. "That's not you," I said to no one in particular. Not anymore. I knelt down and sniffed Baby's neck, hoping to get her aroma one last time. Even that was different. Everything that made Baby distinctive was gone. Her body, once delightful and vibrant, now appeared devoid of purpose. It was like an old piece of clothes left behind, or one of the millions of empty seashells littered across the beach. I felt oddly relaxed about it.

I left my pet and slowly climbed the stairs to my room. Baby's death had put me in an impossible situation. I hated that Mom was upset, but I didn't know what I could do to help her understand. I didn't choose to behave this way. It was simply a reflex, my natural reaction. I suppose I could have faked it. It would have been quite easy for me to appear to be emotional and cry alongside Harlowe. But I did not want to. That would have been a falsehood. And lying was something I had promised my mother I would not do.

The next morning, I was relieved to be at school. Similar to the tranquility I'd had in my room, it was pleasant to be around people who didn't expect me to be sad. My classmates and professors had no idea that Baby had died, so I didn't have to pretend to be sad. I went about my day as if nothing was wrong, because, in my opinion, nothing was.

In the carpool line that afternoon, I was relieved to see my grandmother's car approaching the corner. Mom was undoubtedly still upset, so spending time in the van with my grandmother was a relief. We talked happily on the way home. I imagined my grandmother had not heard about Baby, therefore everything was fine. But, as we approached the corner into our neighborhood, I noticed something strange: Mom's car was parked in the driveway. Why did Grandma pick me up when Mom was home?

I got out of the car and rushed up the walk to our townhouse. Before I could force it open, the door swung quickly inward. My sister stood on the other side, smiling and holding a Popsicle. She handed it to me.

"Welcome home, Kaat!" she exclaimed, using the nickname she had mysteriously given me the previous summer. "Wanna play Barbies?"

I smiled at her and took the popsicle. Over her shoulder, I could see Mom in the kitchen preparing something to eat. She had yet to acknowledge me.

"Mommy," I said as I walked in. "Why didn't you pick me up today?"

Mom did not move from the counter, where she was meticulously chopping a tomato. "Because I was busy with your sister," she explained.

"Doing what?" I said, glancing at Harlowe. "Making Popsicles?"

Mom shook her head and transferred the tomato to a bowl. "We buried Baby, actually."

I froze. Cold wrath surged from the earth and settled in my stomach. I set the Popsicle on the counter, and the crimson dye rapidly stained the white Formica. "Wha—" I stammered. "WHAT?!"

Mom put the knife down and turned around. "Well, you didn't seem like you cared much last night," she remarked, almost smugly, "so I didn't think you'd mind."

Her comment struck me like a punch, and wrath rose to my throat. "You're lying," I murmured gently, almost containing myself. Mom made a step towards me.

"What did you say to me?" she inquired, ready to fire a censure.

I stared at her in the eyes, and her ludicrous reaction made me even furious. Unable to control my rage, I grabbed the nearest object, a glass pitcher, and hurled it as hard as I could against the wall behind her head.

"YOU'RE A LIAR!" I yelled.

The pitcher exploded against the wall, showering my mother with tiny glass pieces. Harlowe began crying. I stomped out of the kitchen and up to my room, becoming more determined with each step. That was enough. I was finished with it. It made no difference whether you were bad or good, honest or dishonest. Everything got me into trouble. And I was tired of attempting to play by rules that were always changing for no apparent reason. From now on, I will do whatever I please. What was I afraid of? Nothing, that's what.

I got it inside my room and closed the door. I had barely a few seconds of silence before the door flung wide and my mother burst in. It wasn't enough time to regain control.

"Patric!" she shrieked. "What is wrong with you?!"

"What's wrong with me?!" I screamed back, quivering with rage. "You took my little sister out of school so you could bury my pet!" I burst into tears. "AND YOU WANT TO KNOW WHAT'S WRONG WITH ME?!"

Mom had a dab of blood on her cheek from being injured by a piece of glass. She wiped at it while taking another step forward. "I assumed you wouldn't care." Only she said it with a lot less confidence.

"Bullshit."

It was the first time I had cursed in front of her, let alone at her. But I didn't care. "You were upset because I did not react the way you expected me to. You were upset because I never respond the way you expect me to." Mom looked down, as my comments struck a chord. "You did this to punish me," I said angrily. "You did this because I'm different."

Mom looked at me. Slivers of glass glistened in her hair, like diamonds. "I thought it would teach you a lesson," she responded, daring to show horror.

"And what lesson is that?" I inquired, coming closer to her. "Should I be more like everyone else?" "More like you?" I laughed sarcastically and shook my head in mock sympathy. "You're a liar who insists everyone else tell the truth," I told you. "You're a cheater who demands everyone else play fair." I paused for emphasis, then hissed, "I'd rather be dead than be like you."

My words fell like the blade of a guillotine. Mom's face turned white, and she backed toward the door. Her expression had turned into this gaze.

"You," she exclaimed, almost able to breathe, "are a nightmare." She yelled, "YOU STAY IN YOUR ROOM!"

She slammed the door and dashed downstairs. I waited long enough to ensure she had left before definitely walking out of my room. As I strolled down the hallway, blood rushed through my veins. It energized me. I loved the confrontation. My family avoided conflict, but I did not. It piqued my interest and was even delicious. It made me feel powerful.

Do you want to take anything from me? I thought as I walked gently into her room. Do you want to take something beautiful and make sure I never see it again? I crossed to the dresser, where she kept her favorite items. "Well, I can do that, too." The top drawer held a set of ruby earrings she'd owned since she was a child. My great-grandmother had given them to her, and they were among her most valuable items. I took them to the bathroom and flushed them.

Back in my room, I leaned against the door and looked at the opposite wall. My fury was evaporating, as was the irritation and tension that had been accumulating since Baby's death. I didn't feel anything. Only now, like inside the abandoned house, did I like the feeling of nothingness. It was relaxing. I wanted to embrace it.

With my mother already enraged, I didn't have to worry about "right" or "wrong" reactions. I didn't have to worry about the tension that came with attempting to act normally. Alone in my room, I didn't have to fake reactions to show emotions I didn't feel. I was free of all emotions, expectations, and pressures!

"I can just be myself," I muttered.

A sentence from "Who Framed Roger Rabbit?" sprang to mind. "I'm not bad," Jessica Rabbit explains. "I'm just drawn that way." I can sympathize. I, too, was simply drawn that way. I wasn't attempting to damage anyone or cause trouble. I only wanted to make my mother understand.

"It is not my fault that I do not feel the same way as everyone else. So, what should I do? I looked at my bed and realized I was exhausted. I sank on top of my comforter.

Several hours later, I awoke with a start. My bedroom was dark, and the entire house was silent. What's happening? I thought. What time is it? Then I remembered. The ferret. The fight. The earrings. I sighed and rolled to my side. Harlowe was sleeping on the bed next to me. It was after midnight. Mom must have come in at some time and put her to bed. I massaged my face and sat up, realizing the magnitude of the issue.

The sound of whispering interrupted my focus. The voices came from my mother's chamber. She was on the phone. "I was only trying to get a reaction," she explained, crying gently into the receiver. "I know I did it the wrong way, but I don't know what to do. She does not appear to be feeling. "She doesn't seem to care about anything!"

My thoughts raced. I entered the hallway and sneaked up to Mom's door, hugging the wall so she couldn't see me.

"Baby died," she added. "Harlowe has been beyond herself with sadness since the incident. What about Patric? Nothing! And that is not all! This afternoon, she hurled a pitcher at me. Last month, they phoned me from school because she had locked some students in a bathroom. "I don't know what to do!"

I grimaced. I had forgotten about the bathroom. The strain at school that day was tremendous. It had been building for weeks, and no terrible behavior seemed to alleviate the tension. In class, I felt like I couldn't breathe. The room felt like it was shrinking, and a familiar worry sprang to mind: "What if it doesn't stop?" It was a question that lingered in my mind. In the back of my mind, I wondered what would happen if I couldn't keep the pressure under control. I thought about the men inside the prison, then remembered the day I stabbed Syd—how fast the tension had subsided and how fantastic it felt in the aftermath—and tried to drive the temptation of that relief away from my mind.

No, I replied to myself. No. No, no.

My skull felt swollen as I fidgeted violently in class. I excused myself to the bathroom, hoping that getting some fresh air would help clear my head. A gaggle of sixth-grade girls shuffled along the corridor ahead of me. They were also going to the bathroom, and when they got inside, the huge metal door slammed shut behind them.

I stood outside the door. Above the handle was a deadbolt that locked from the outside. I'd always found it fascinating. Why would you want to lock a restroom from the outside? But, more importantly, what will happen if I do?

The corridor served as a breezeway, and the air felt cool as I stepped forward. I wrapped my fingers around the huge deadbolt, noticing how small my hand appeared against the metal handle. Was I strong enough to wrench such a lock? Initially, I couldn't. Then I remembered that our patio sliders needed to be pushed slightly forward for the bolt to catch. Leaning against the door, I felt the tumbler start to turn. I carefully turned it till I heard it click in place. Then I stepped back.

The females only realized they were locked after a short time, but it felt like an eternity. It reminded me of bouncing on the large trampoline in gym class. My favorite part was the millisecond when I had soared as far as I could but hadn't yet begun to fall back down. It was a unique form of freedom. In an instant, all of the pressure was gone. In its stead, I felt peaceful. I had a high. This time, nobody was bleeding.

The females began knocking on the door and screaming. I listened to them with a distant interest. Why would somebody be terrified of being trapped in a bathroom? I was thinking about this when I was interrupted by a voice from down the hallway.

"What exactly is going on here?"

I swung around to face Mrs. Genereaux, the sixth-grade teacher. She ran by me, quickly unlocking the deadbolt. The girls burst out, their faces drenched with tears.

"Did you do this?" she questioned, almost shouting at me. "Did you lock this door?"

The contrast between the deep tranquility in which I had just recently been engrossed and the chaotic situation unfolding in the corridor made me uncommonly negligent. I tried to stammer out a denial, but it was ineffective. My guilt was evident. Mrs. Genereaux grabbed my wrist and marched me to the principal's office before I could say anything else.

Later, while I sat next to the reception counter, waiting for my mother to come retrieve me, I had a strange sense of confusion. I'd never been caught like that. I wasn't thinking, just rationalizing. The danger of allowing the pressure to increase for so long became clear. It made me sloppy, I recognized soberly. It made me dangerous.

I recalled the men incarcerated and Officer Bobby's remark when I inquired if all sociopaths ended up in jail. "Probably," he replied. "Unless they're really smart."

That's what I need to be, I am determined. Very smart.

Inflicting pain (or suffering) was a guaranteed, immediate technique of pressure relief. I wasn't sure why. All I knew was that the release from stabbing Syd was the best sensation I'd ever experienced. It wasn't simply that I didn't care. It was that I didn't care. I was a kite soaring high in the sky, free of strain and stress, as well as any emotional expectations. Yet, I understood there was a risk in permitting myself to do something so immoral. For starters, it was risky. Even worse, it was addictive.

Even though I was young, I recognized that so much of my energy was spent attempting to keep the strain at bay. Succumbing to my worst compulsions was simple and needed no effort. God, I adored that release. It seemed as if I could float on a tide of acquiescence. Is there a term for this feeling?

"Surrender."

The word emerged on my lips as if said by someone else, and I knew it was correct. I was also confused. What do you surrender to? I wondered. My darker side? What about my "bad" urges?

I stood outside Mom's bedroom, desperate to understand. My thoughts were interrupted as she cried into the phone. "I'm afraid," she said. "I might have to send her to boarding school."

My eyes expanded. Boarding school? She fell silent when the person on the other end spoke. I sighed and lowered my head.

To be fair, I had always had a secret ambition to be sent to boarding school. Miss Porter's School in Connecticut, for example, seemed like an ideal destination to spend my adolescence. After all, I was about to enter junior high. I hadn't quite figured out the specifics, but I could picture myself in a pristine plaid uniform with nicely plaited braids concealing dozens of lock-friendly bobby pins. I considered it a fresh start. A fresh location in which I could hide in plain sight. It sounded amazing. Nonetheless, I despised the idea of abandoning my mother. Despite what I'd said in fury and the peace I felt after our quarrel, I loved my mother. I was wary of a world without her leadership, even as I slowly began to realize that her advice was an illusion. It would never really apply to someone like me.

Why doesn't she simply get it? I thought, annoyed. Maybe if I didn't feel like I had to continually pretend to be like everyone else and hide from everyone else, I wouldn't be so stressed. Maybe I wouldn't feel the pressure. I wouldn't have the impulse to be bad. Why doesn't she understand?

I went to bed exhausted. A window on the wall across from me looked out at a fence and the ocean beyond it. I looked through the window and saw a cat walking along the top of the fence.

CHAPTER 5

ESTATE PLANNING

I met David at a summer camp when I was fourteen.

My mother enrolled me in a creative arts program after I declined to accompany Harlowe to church camp. "You're not going to spend the summer sitting alone at home all day," she'd told you. "So either you go to camp or you start coming to work with me."

Surprisingly, I loved it. The event was held in what had been one of oil billionaire John D. Rockefeller's winter houses. A few weeks after arriving, I heard rumors that Rockefeller had personally overseen the construction of a network of secret tunnels beneath the house that connected to numerous buildings throughout town. I became captivated with the rumor and needed to discover whether it was real.

There was a drawer in the administration office full of house-related documentation. Determined to get my hands on them, I began spending all of my free time there. I was loitering inside one day, waiting for an opportunity to spy, when an achingly attractive boy passed through the door.

"How's it going?" he inquired.

I was momentarily speechless. David was somewhat taller than me, with hair that matched his dark brown eyes and a deep tan accented by a plain white T-shirt. He wore faded peach board shorts and carried a large ACA Joe duffel bag over his shoulder. I wondered whether I was little enough to fit inside so he could carry me wherever he went.

"Patric," the camp director exclaimed as she entered the office, interrupting my strange daydream. "This is David. "Today is his first day."

"Cool," I responded as calmly as I could.

The camp director walked into an internal office and left us alone. David grinned at me. I switched my attention to the drawer containing the historical records. I seized the opportunity, hastily opening it and removing a set of blueprints. Then I returned my attention to David, smiling broadly as I slipped the ancient paperwork into my bag.

"First time here?" I inquired.

He looked at me suspiciously and responded, "Yeah…"

The camp director walked back inside. She gave him a welcome kit and a map of the property. "Patric," she asked, "would you mind showing David around?"

"Of course," I responded.

"You're in good hands, young man," the director remarked, smiling. "Patric probably knows her way around here better than I do!"

She was correct. Obsessed with the tunnel story, I had spent the last few weeks exploring the entire estate. Typically, I made my ventures during lunch breaks or after hours when no one else was watching. But, thanks to David's surprise arrival, I had an excuse to stroll the grounds without asking any questions.

We roamed the property together. With my notebook in hand, I meticulously described all three stories of the mansion, noting the rooms and structures that matched the drawings.

"You sure are thorough," David commented. It was an hour into his "tour" and I still hadn't shown him any camp-related aspects of the land.

"Well, it's a complex layout," I stated as I led him down another corridor of closed doors. "It's important to know how to get around."

"Still, I'm not sure I need to see every one of these rooms." Then he continued, "I don't mind. It isn't every day that I get to walk with such a lovely girl."

His words caught me off guard. Nobody outside of my family has ever called me lovely. I stared at David with curiosity. He made such a strong statement, and I reasoned that it revealed more about him than it did about me.

I smiled and lifted my brows before folding my arms across my chest. "Can you keep a secret?" I asked. I moved to a nearby conference room and motioned for him to follow. Inside, I lay the drawings on the table and told him all about the hidden tunnels and my goal to find out whether the stories were correct. Involving others in my idea was hazardous and uncharacteristic of me. However, something about David made me want to tell him everything.

After that, we were inseparable. David was entering his senior year, a few classes ahead of me. He worked two jobs to support his mother and sister. He smoked cigarettes, used a phony ID, and drove his own automobile, which he purchased with his own money. And, like me, he was ready to break the rules when he felt they didn't make sense. However, beneath his rebellious surface, he was a straight-A student, a gentle and compassionate spirit unlike anyone I'd ever encountered. I was objective and cold, but David was emotional and impassioned.

My feelings for David, while powerful, were difficult for me to understand at first. Granted, most of my knowledge of teenage love came from V.C. Andrews' writings. And, while I was relieved to discover that my sentiments were not incestuous nor turbulent, they were also difficult to fully internalize.

My emotional constitution appeared to be similar to a cheap set of crayons. I have access to the primary colors: pleasure and melancholy. However, more nuanced hues—complex sensations such as romantic love and passion—were always beyond my reach. I knew such things existed because I'd read about them in books and seen examples on television, but I'd never been able to identify with them.

In school, we read Wuthering Heights. The girls in class swooned over Heathcliff and professed a strong bond with Catherine "Cathy" Earnshaw, the female protagonist who falls (and eventually goes insane) for him. To them, the book was a gripping star-crossed lovers tragedy. But I didn't get it.

The night I finished, I sighed and tossed the book under the couch, casting a scowl at my mother. "You didn't like it?" she inquired. "Why not?"

"Because Cathy's an idiot," I answered. "She's Heather," I said, referring to the iconic 1980s film. "She acts 'unruly' and 'crazy,' but it's all for show; all she wants is prestige and a dull husband. Meanwhile, she is collapsing and sobbing over Heathcliff. She does not even understand Heathcliff." I rolled my eyes. "He's no prize, either, by the way." I shook my head and remarked, "I can't believe that book is supposed to be the epitome of love stories. I'd kill myself if I behaved like that."

"Just wait 'til you meet someone you really like," Mom said.

Then suddenly, I did. But it was not like Wuthering Heights.

My sentiments for David were neither obsessive nor possessive; they were effortless. I wasn't out of control or delirious as Cathy was with Heathcliff. He didn't "sweep me off my feet," however. My feet were firmly rooted. Perhaps for the first time in my life. But the best part was that I had a pretty cool individual with his feet right next to mine—the coolest person in the world, in my opinion. Meeting David was like finally answering a complicated mystery. Oh, I thought, this is how it works for me.

In terms of romance, David represented more than just everything I wanted. He embodied everything I aspired to be. He could access and express a wide range of emotions, yet he never made me feel bad because I couldn't. Being with David made me feel complete. I no longer felt compelled to keep my "dark" secrets to myself. His acceptance made me feel comfortable, as if I could talk to him about anything.

"This is bullshit," I exclaimed, irritated.

It was late afternoon, and we had sneaked out of an art class to look for a door on the blueprints. We hadn't been able to find it, and now we know why. The intended location for the door was in the center of what had become a commercial kitchen, and it was obscured by an immense china cabinet that took up half the wall.

"There is no way we will be able to move this," I grumbled. I dropped to the floor and flashed my flashlight below the hutch. Despite my limited vantage point, I could plainly see the base of what appeared to be a thin wooden door. "David!" I whispered excitedly, bending my head to get a closer look. "It's here!"

He did not respond. He sat in a corner of the room, his attention focused on something in his lap. I shone my flashlight at him. "David!" I whispered again, but this time louder. "Did you listen to what I said? "I can see the door."

"Shhhhhh," he replied. He held his beloved Swiss Army knife. "I'm cutting my hair," he explained gently.

"What does that even mean?" I inquired with an annoyed sigh. "We don't have time for this!"

David lifted himself from the floor and approached the cabinets. Then, measuring up the massive cupboard, he carefully tipped it backward. "Make yourself useful," he said. "Hold this for me."

I raced to my feet to hold the cabinet in place. "It's really easy," he explained, kneeling down. "The fabric reduces friction."

My jaw fell as I saw him attach the soft material to the cabinet's feet. God, he was intelligent. And resourceful! David spent a few weeks each summer loading freight for his father's trucking company in Boston, so he was well-versed in the art of transportation. He seemed to be knowledgeable about everything.

Our skill sets were a wonderful complement. Whereas I could tell a falsehood or lift a wallet, David was well-versed in history and physics, as well as possessing an extraordinary capacity for problem solving.

He's the yang to my yin, I thought, as I watched him attach the final piece of felt. He had trimmed the fabric into tiny squares, making them almost unnoticeable. Unless you were looking directly at the cabinet's feet, you wouldn't notice they were there. He shifted to the side and pushed. With its new felt feet, the cabinet slipped from the wall with no effort. A thin wooden door stood there, exactly where the drawings predicted.

Giving David an enthusiastic look, I slowly twisted the knob until it clicked. The door's hinges creaked loudly as it opened. We stood transfixed, waiting to see if anyone had heard. Then, once we were certain the coast was clear, we pushed through the frame and disappeared into darkness. I adjusted my flashlight.

As we suspected, the door opened right into a series of crumbling stairs that led sharply down. The dimly lit stairs led to another doorway, the frame of which was horribly bent, as if a giant had wrenched it from its hinges and hurled it to the side.

"Creepy," David commented. I smiled. We carefully descended the stairs and ducked under the bent frame into what appeared to be a massive unfinished space approximately the size of the entire first floor of the house. I searched the chamber with my flashlight, and we both gasped when it revealed an archway in the corner, blocked by a thick layer of bricks. There was a hefty iron chain across it. I rushed over and ran my palm across the reddish blocks. They appeared fresher than the ones that framed the rest of the basement. This had to be it, I reasoned, taking a step back. "And even if it's not," I said, "I'm gonna say that it is."

David was just behind me. He gave me a bear embrace and yelled, "Holy crap! "You did it!" He spun me around to face him and exclaimed, "You found the tunnel!"

Then he kissed me.

Surprised, I took a fast inhale, which enhanced the flavor. He tasted like smokey dark chocolate with hints of tobacco. "Hungry" was how they described it. I was hungry, voracious for what? I did not know. I placed one hand on the small of his back. The flesh was heated. He pressed me close to his chest, and I wished I could crawl under his T-shirt. Then I dropped the lamp, and we were plunged into darkness.

On the last day of camp, I made my way to the kitchen. I had hidden the plans I had taken from the director's office beneath the china cabinet. As I drew them from their hiding spot, I smiled, recalling the first time I saw them.

"You gonna put those back?" David yelled out abruptly from the doorway.

I smiled. "Yes," I said dutifully. "I was going on my way out."

"Is your mom almost here?" he inquired, nodding.

I shrugged, rolling my eyes. He volunteered to drive me home, but to our dismay, Mom refused.

"You are a fourteen-year-old girl," she remarked when I called to inquire. "And he is what? Is it almost eighteen? "Certainly not."

I was disappointed. We'd spent almost every day this summer together. What was the point of such a short drive? But David understood and, like a gentleman, insisted on staying while I waited for her.

"Yes, she'll be here soon," I replied.

He stared down at the floor. I could see he was sad.

"Hey," I said. "What's up with you?"

"What do you think?" he said, a little too forcefully. "I'm gonna miss you."

I gave him an exaggerated pout before crossing the room and throwing my arms around his waist. "Awww," I purred. "But you don't live too far away. "We'll see each other all the time."

"Not really," he replied.

"What are you talking about?" I asked. "You have a car."

"Yeah, a car your mom says you're never allowed to get in." As we embraced, he remained silent. When I looked up at him, I noticed an expression that was both sad and enraged. "What does it matter?" he asked. "We attend different schools. And next year, I'll be in college. He adjusted his weight and shook his head, as if attempting to stabilize himself. "I mean, you're only in junior high…"

A familiar feeling of worry crept into my chest. I pushed away from him. "Wrong," I snapped. "I am about to start high school. And since when are you concerned about that?"

I was becoming angry. We had been dating for weeks, and David had never mentioned my age or the fact that we attended separate schools. He was using that as justification for what? Dumping me? It did not make sense. Not knowing what else to do, I decided to change tactics.

"Besides," I said in my romantic Moonlighting voice, "you said you wanted to come explore my neighborhood."

It was a last-ditch attempt to shake him out of whatever was dragging him down. For a little while, it appeared to work. He began to smile and shifted his large brown eyes up to meet mine.

"That does sound fun," he admitted.

"See?" I replied by throwing my arms around his waist once again. I gently kissed him on the cheek. "How am I supposed to stay safe without you around?"

One of the administrators stuck her head inside the room. "Hey!" she exclaimed sharply. "You lovebirds aren't supposed to be here." She scowled at David. "Besides, Patric, your mom's here."

"I gotta go," he whispered gently, and I realized my spell had been shattered.

"Wait," I replied. I pleaded with the administration. "Can you give us, like, two seconds please?"

"You can have all the time you want in the lobby."

"No, it's okay," David said. He kissed my cheek and said, "I'll see ya."

Then he went out the door.

CHAPTER 6

POPS OF COLOR

I decided to apply to UCLA in my junior year of high school.

"It's a little late to apply to an out-of-state school," my guidance counselor, Mrs. Rodriguez, had remarked.

I sat across from the woman at her desk. Behind her was a framed poster of a man standing in front of many Lamborghini cars. It said "Justification for Higher Education," and I wanted to toss it out the window.

She looked at my grades and said, "Out-of-state applicants are advised to start the process early."

I already despised Mrs. Rodriguez. Despite her predilection for Easter-hued ill-fitting pantsuits, I could tell she was an aggressive rule follower. She was also extremely pessimistic, the worst possible combo.

"Actually," I answered excitedly, "my father lives in California." So I'll be considered in-state." I didn't mean to be argumentative, but Mrs. Rodriguez appeared to want to slap me. She shifted in her seat and began playing with a caterpillar-shaped rhinestone pin that glittered cruelly from her purple lapel.

"Well, I don't know about any of that," she said. "But I don't think it makes sense to apply to UCLA this late in the game, especially when there are so many good colleges just in your own backyard! After all, how would you react if you learned that a California student was applying to the University of Florida as an in-state candidate?" she asked.

I was positive I would not care at all. I wasn't about to take life advice from a woman whose sense of "success' ' consisted of buying outmoded sports cars on a regular basis. But I wasn't going to discuss that with Mrs. Rodriguez.

My decision to attend UCLA was based entirely on distance, not academics. As a youngster nearing maturity, I was no closer to figuring out what made me so different. Worse, I hadn't been able to find less damaging ways to deal with it. I knew I'd been lucky thus far. Throughout middle and high school, I found covert outlets for my gloom, such as late-night stalkings and empty-house excursions. But the balancing act proved challenging. My luck would eventually run out in the small, conservative community where I lived.

What I need is a big city, I reasoned, visualizing a setting where invisibility would not take constant effort, where I might hide in plain sight. Then one night, it occurred to me. Los Angeles! The city where my father now lived provided me with a luxury I had only dreamed of: automatic invisibility. With its enormous territory and millions of citizens, I could be anyone in Los Angeles. I could blend in. I could disappear.

My mother was not pleased with the thought of me relocating across the country for education. But, for a variety of reasons, I insisted. Although I loved my family, I felt I needed to leave—for their sake as well as mine. This was especially true for my sister, whose ability to see behind my "good girl" facade had become a source of concern.

"Look at this," she told me one afternoon.

It was Saturday and we were in the den. Harlowe sat on the couch, scribbling in her sketchbook as I played a computer game. My sister enjoyed drawing and had developed into an excellent cartoonist. She dropped her most recent effort in front of me, a character she'd invented. In the center of the page, she drew a giant "A" and a masked female superhero wearing a cape. "CAPTAIN APATHY," the caption read. "For Untruth, Injustice, and the Anarchist's Way."

I examined the image of the caped crusader and the words she had put to the speech bubble above her head. "Have no fear!" she stated. "Captain Apathy does not care!"

"Whoa," I replied gently. I was uncharacteristically silent. Harlowe grinned.

"It's you," she announced triumphantly. "My favorite superhero is Kaat!" Then she skipped happily into the kitchen to make her favorite snack, delicately microwaved Chips Ahoy!" cookies. I sat down and peered grimly at the cartoon. I wasn't sure what made me different from everyone else, but I knew I wasn't a superhero.

If anything, Harlowe was my hero—a naturally wonderful person. She didn't have any demons to face, secrets to keep, or harmful drives to overcome. It was almost as if I was born with an extra dose of darkness. Her dosage. Harlowe had pure lightness, whereas I had a predisposition for mischief. I had always known our differences were sharp, but Captain Apathy made it clear that I wasn't alone.

Fortunately, college offered the appropriate solution. If I moved away, I wouldn't have to worry about hiding from my mother or infecting my sister. I could live life on my own terms. Without anything to protest against, I wondered whether my destructive impulses would go away. I suspected they would.

Maybe I could simply be average.

The words struck me like a bolt of lightning one night, and I couldn't shake them off. The prospect of such a life, free of dark cravings and growing tensions, was always on my mind. I had been thinking about it for as long as I could remember, but I knew better than to get my hopes up. Until then.

Maybe once I get to college, everything will change.

Initially, it was the case. Life in Los Angeles was pleasant, if not mundane. Dad drove me up at the airport the day I arrived, and we spent the next few weeks seeing UCLA and settling me into my dorm. My room was on the second floor of a renovated sorority home that overlooked Hilgard Avenue. It had floor-to-ceiling French doors and the sole ornate balcony in the home. I loved it.

I had the place all to myself for the first three days. I had been allocated a suitemate—her name was chalked in chalk next to mine on the door—but I had no idea who she was or when she would come. As the days passed, I hoped she would never appear. But my hopes for solitary life were dashed when, the day before courses began, the door swung open and a lovely Chinese girl carrying several enormous luggage strode across the threshold.

"Hello, my name is Patric," I said gently.

The girl looked at me with stunning wide almond eyes. Then she reached into her huge purse. After exploring for a few seconds, she discovered a small silver box the size of a graphing calculator. It featured a speaker on one end and a microphone on the other. She swiftly talked into the box, her Mandarin message translated to English by a monotone masculine voice that exploded aggressively from its speaker: "Nice to meet you, my name is Kimi."

"A translator!"" I glanced at the magical box. "Do you take this wherever you go?"The box relayed my message to Kimi, who nodded happily. Kimi was an overseas student. She'd never visited the United States and did not speak English.

"Translator, yes," Kimi replied. "Machine." She patted the box.

"Well, it's nice to meet you, Kimi," I commented. Then I addressed the box: "And you as well, Machine."

I pictured a room with a view and a roommate who couldn't speak to me. Life could not have been more wonderful. At first, I was pleasantly overloaded by classes and assignments. I enjoyed being busy. When I wasn't studying or sitting in class, I spent my time roaming the campus. My enormous course load, along with the novelty of my surroundings, depleted all of my mental energy. Each night, I collapsed into bed and slipped into a deep sleep, waking up rejuvenated and relaxed the next morning. It was fantastic. It was powerful. It was usual. But it did not last long.

After the first semester, progress stalled. I felt myself dragged into typical sensations of restlessness and lethargy now that the hustle of acclimatization had subsided. I could feel the increasing pressure and intense stress that always seemed to accompany it. I still had my newfound freedom, but the peace had vanished. Without anything to distract me, I discovered that my destructive impulses were still very much alive. And, without the convenience of my childhood bedroom window, I had to find alternative creative outlets.

My favorite area was Sigma Phi Epsilon's dining room. It included inner pocket doors with windows that provided mainly unobstructed views of the other common areas, as well as floor-to-ceiling glass sliders that looked out onto the backyard. As long as the doors were closed and the lights were turned out, I could watch individuals from two different angles for hours. The major reason I was so excited to attend the party on Saturday was that it was held at the Sigma house. People-watching from my hiding position sounded like a great way to spend the evening. As soon as I arrived, I dashed to the dining room to claim my position. But on the way there, I was knocked down by a very inebriated fraternity mate.

"Oh, no!" He stammered, regained his footing, and awkwardly attempted to help me up. "I'm so sorry! Are you OK?"

"Yeah, it's no problem," I responded, taking my purse.

"I'm Steve," he murmured, his tired eyes blinking slowly. Unlike most sober partygoers, I enjoyed mingling with drunks. Their memories of me the following morning would be foggy, at best. It was kind of like being a ghost.

Steve smiled and pointed an unsteady finger at my chest. "Hey." He paused. "Don't I know you?""

"No," I replied, chuckling.

"Yeah," he repeated, as if I hadn't spoken. "You're Sarah."

I said nothing and was shocked as he placed his body against mine, my back against the corridor wall. Steve's lips touched my ear. "Guess what?"He whispered. "I am out of cigarettes. He murmured, "Go get us some, and I'll owe you forever."

He took an awkward step back and pressed a set of keys on my hand. I stood there, unsure what to do. Steve nodded and pointed his finger at me again, mistaking my perplexity for resistance in some unwritten agreement I had no role in.

"Right," he muttered, reaching into his pocket and handing me a large wallet. "Gotcha. "Get whatever you want," Steve stated. He grinned and stumbled back down the hall toward the living room. He sank into a couch in a state of semi consciousness.

I examined the keys and wallet in my hand. Only moments ago, I had intended to spend the evening alone in a dark room, observing other people interact. And that was okay. But this was way better!

The automobile was easy to find. I raised the keys above my head and walked around the parking lot, pushing unlock on the fob. Steve's Acura's lights eventually blinked from a corner parking place. I opened the door and tossed my purse and Steve's wallet in. I eased into the driver's seat and inserted the key into the ignition. I sat for a time, taking in my unexpected good fortune. Then I started driving.

I took Sunset to the shore and then turned north on the Pacific Coast Highway, cruising for miles alongside the ocean. When I reached the mountains hugging the Malibu shoreline, I turned right and drove through Calabasas before entering the San Fernando Valley suburbs. I drove for over an hour down Ventura Boulevard, then through the Hollywood Hills before returning to the UCLA campus via the Beverly Hills flats.

It was almost two a.m. when I finally stopped at a store. I figured it was the prudent thing to do. I grabbed a sleeve of Starbursts and approached the counter. The cigarettes were locked in a glass case behind the cash register. I asked the cashier for the brand that matched the empty packs I'd seen crumpled on the car floor and handed him Steve's credit card. I didn't expect him to ask for my ID, but to be safe, I distracted him with some charm. I leaned forward and casually touched the back of my hand against his wrist, looking him directly in the eyes.

"What is the weirdest thing you've seen while working here this late?I inquired, genuinely curious.

The cashier was caught off surprise. "The craziest thing?" He ran the card through the scanner, then handed it back to me, deep in thought. Then his face lightened up. "One time I helped a lady get away from a guy chasing her," he remembered saying.

"Holy shit!"" I replied, astonished. "Good on you!" I grabbed the cigarettes and called, "Have a good night!" over my shoulder as I departed.

A short time later, I carefully returned the Acura to its location on fraternity row. I knew my trip had ended, but I couldn't bring myself to open the door. The car felt like a decompression chamber. Driving across town in Steve's automobile was exhilarating—just the emotional boost I needed. I sat quietly in the darkness, noticing as all of my emotions faded away. The effect made me feel drowsy. I slipped into my seat. U2's The Joshua Tree was played from Steve's CD player. I closed my eyes and silently created my own version of one of the verses.

"She will suffer the feeling of thrill / She's running to stand still."

That's exactly how it seemed, as if my need for a splash of color had nothing to do with emotion. Rather, it was designed to exhaust my emotional experience, allowing me to stand still—to experience apathy without pressure or stuck stress.

"So if right now I feel comfortably apathetic," I pondered, "then what tips the scale? What causes it to be uncomfortable?" I reflected on how stuck stress always accompanied the pressure, as well as the claustrophobic worry it mirrored. Then I shook my head, frustrated. "How can someone be anxious and apathetic at the same time?"

I was in too good a mood to consider it. I forced these questions from my head and glanced drowsily out the window. I sat there contentedly for a few more minutes before removing the keys from the ignition. I put them, together with the cigarettes and money, into the passenger seat. Then I got out and headed back to my hostel, already planning how I would do it again. It did not take long for me to devise a plan.

That unexpected joyride was the first of many. In the months that followed, I embarked on scores more midnight excursions, but they became increasingly purposeful. I discovered that I was less drowsy on days when I knew I'd shortly be driving around the city in someone else's automobile. The anticipation of the excitement, rather than the act itself, relieved my anxiety.

I was less concerned about my compulsions once I realized what was motivating them—that, as Dr. Slack put it, I was unconsciously motivated to do anything, anything, to raise my apathetic baseline. They had normalized. "Normalization is a therapeutic tool through which a state of mind or belief system previously thought to be anomalous or irregular is redefined as 'normal,'" Dr. Slack explained, underlining the word on her chalkboard. "Normalizing mental disorders—specifically the various symptoms of mental disorders— is essential to counteracting the stigma associated with those symptoms and replacing it with knowledge, understanding and, eventually, acceptance."

This explanation spoke to me deeply and caused a significant shift in my psychological understanding. Although I realized that my destructive tendencies were not "normal" in the broad sense, I discovered that they were common among people like me.

So I'm not crazy, I reasoned.

The relief was unexpected and profound. Although I never allowed it to dominate my thoughts, I had always been uncomfortable with the variances in my personality type. The worst part was not understanding anything, especially my destructive tendencies. Now that I knew what had triggered them, I could better manage my reactions to them. All I had to do was wait until the weekend.

On Friday and Saturday nights, practically all of the UCLA Greek groups would throw large parties down Frat Row. I'd go down the narrow street, looking for the house with the loudest and most disorderly party. Then I'd walk inside, zero in on the most inebriated occupant, and find a method to skillfully remove him from his car keys. Sometimes I drove quickly, sometimes I drove slowly. I would travel a long distance some nights and only a few blocks others. The only continuous aspects of such journeys were the relaxation that came from alleviating the burden of apathy and the satisfaction that came from knowing that I'd found a dependable, if temporary, remedy.

I realized the probable ramifications of my actions. If detected in a stolen car, arrest and perhaps jail time were quite likely results. But I was not disturbed. That's the trouble with individuals like me, I reasoned as I drove my sleek BMW through the take-out lane of the Westwood In-N-Out Burger. We do not care. Incarceration was not something I feared; rather, it was almost an incentive. Officer Bobby's detainees were safe from themselves, as far as I remembered. A brief spell in prison sounded intriguing.

Without anything to stimulate me and no route out, I wondered if I'd still desire emotional flashes of color. Or will my black-and-white interior world become more manageable? A part of me wanted to find out. However, I knew I was unlikely to get caught. None of the guys ever reported their autos as stolen. In most cases, the keys were freely provided, if not soberly. They were always too intoxicated at the time to recall having a car, let alone realize it was gone. Even if one of them realized their car was missing and that I had taken it, I knew exactly how I would explain things.

"Here are your chips, handsome." I threw a bag of Doritos at my latest target, who was sprawled on top of a beanbag in the living room of his frat home. He opened his eyes and wiped his forehead, anxiously attempting to concentrate.

"Hey, pretty," he whispered, smiling. "Where have you gone?"

"To get you some chips, like you asked," I said softly, bending down to kiss him on the cheek. "Here are your keys," I threw them at him. "See ya later." Like every previous unwitting victim, I had no desire in talking to the boy. I was exhausted and comfortable after a night of joyriding. All I wanted to do was get back to my dorm and go to bed. I made it out the door before he could catch me.

The night air was cold, but I didn't mind. It reminded me of when I walked home from the San Francisco slumber party. The streets were deserted, and the residences were quiet. The night was filled with possibilities. When I arrived at my dorm, I skirted the front entrance. I had missed curfew, and after midnight, all the outdoor doors were shut. The only way to get in was to contact the resident advisor. Naturally, I had no intention of informing anyone about my nocturnal pattern. I had made other arrangements before leaving that night.

I always ensured that the window in the maintenance closet at the back of the building was unlocked. I placed my palm on the glass and pushed it gently. Then I lifted the sash, pushed myself up onto the ledge, and crawled inside. As I approached the stairs on the first floor, it was dark. I swiftly climbed to the second floor and tiptoed across the landing to my room. Fluorescent panels flooded the corridor with bright light, and I opened the door as carefully as possible to avoid waking my roommate.

CHAPTER 7

PRESCRIPTION

A few months later, I completed my first year at UCLA.

"You should come home," my mother had said over the phone.

I had wanted to. After all, I wouldn't have anywhere to live when the dorms closed for the summer, and I hadn't seen her or Harlowe in a long time. But with the gravity of my actions on my mind, I knew it wasn't a good idea.

I realized I needed to study more so that I could gain control of myself.

Instead, I decided to move in with my father. His Coldwater Canyon Cape Cod-style home was the most logical option. With its tall white gates and glittering backyard pool, I found serenity within my own little fortress. At least I did at first. But, much like it did when I first came to school, my restlessness returned fast.

I should find a job, I reasoned one afternoon as I examined the set of keys my neighbors had left next to their car, so I don't end up in jail. It was hardly the first time I had contemplated it. Summer vacation lasted from June to September, and it was a genuine workshop of idle hours that my devilish side longed to exploit. These extended months, with their lack of structure and duty, were a smorgasbord of potential calamities for someone like me. And I needed to establish some guidelines.

Although my appointment with Dr. Slack was at first upsetting, it led to an unexpected resolution. The day following the balcony incident, I went back to the library. But that time, I stayed for hours, reading every psychology book and research study I could find on sociopathy.

Days spent in the library after school stretched into weeks as I reflected on the scarcity of resources available to sociopaths. Most of the material I discovered was unsatisfactory. The disorder's descriptions were ambiguous at best and misleading at worst. With few exceptions, the media consistently portrays sociopaths as heinous criminals. Some even advocated sociopathic solitude, which I felt to be extremely frightening. "These people should be avoided at all costs," one vehement magazine article declared.

Where should sociopaths go for help? I wondered. Ultimately, these were human beings. They were in serious need of therapy. However, most of the literature portrayed them as monsters who should be exiled. Sociopaths have been constantly labeled as "evil," "terrible" persons in popular culture, which is mostly based on sensationalized composites and secondhand accounts. They were said to lack conscience. They were believed to lack soul. The books I found stated that sociopaths could not be treated or controlled. They were entirely unpredictable, emotionless, and a threat to society. They lacked self-awareness and emotional growth skills.

But the facts revealed a different reality. Deep in the research racks, I discovered numerous studies demonstrating that not all sociopaths were monsters bent on destruction. Rather, they were persons whose natural temperament made internalizing learned social emotions such as empathy and guilt more challenging, albeit not impossible. This made sense to me based on my personal experiences.

Everything I read indicated that I was a sociopath. I lacked empathy. I was proficient in deception. I was capable of doing violence without remorse. Manipulation came easily. I was superficially appealing. I engaged in criminal activity. I struggled to connect with emotions. I never felt guilty. Nonetheless, I knew I wasn't the monster the media portrayed. I also noticed that my symptoms did not quite match those on Cleckley's psychopathy checklist.

The sociopathic personality was said to be uniformly characterized by "unreliability" and "failure to follow any life plan" (numbers four and sixteen on the list, respectively). However, they could not be applied to me. I was really dependable when I needed to be. I was a decent student who had been very disciplined in order to get into UCLA. Yes, I was often dishonest and insincere (number five). I also lacked empathy and realized I wasn't dealing with a complete emotional deck. But that was the point. I noticed these items. I was aware. I did not suffer any "specific loss of insight" (number 11). That indicated I was capable of not only self-awareness, but also evolution, something the literature claimed sociopaths could not do.

Something wasn't right. From my perspective, the research was grossly inadequate. If everyone was utilizing Cleckley's psychopathy checklist to identify sociopathy, it seemed likely that key details were being omitted. Determined to get to the bottom of it, I began to devote practically all of my free time to researching sociopathy in order to better understand and normalize myself. The seeds of this self-normalization became stronger over time as I realized—not just anecdotally, but empirically—that I wasn't "wrong" or "bad," but different. Like Jessica Rabbit. This dichotomy was especially significant to my concept of love.

According to number nine on Cleckley's list, psychopaths had a "incapacity for love," which was a difficult pill to take. Unfortunately, my lack of meaningful relationships (other than those with my family) seemed to indicate that this trait might apply to me. But when I started thinking about it, I realized it couldn't be. What about David? I wondered.

I recall the night I realized this, and the flood of relief that ensued. It was a couple weeks till spring break. I was sitting in my hostel, reading a book about psychopaths, when it hit me.

"DAVID!"I yelled.

I threw my hand down on the desk, startled Kimi, who had just come back from a shower. She stared at me.

"David!"I said it again. I got up and dashed towards her, placing my hands on her still-damp shoulders. "David was my boyfriend!" And we were in love. Really in love!"

I was exaggerating my outburst. I enjoyed making Kimi stress out. Something about it pleased me beyond the limits of rational thought.

"That sounds nice," Kimi replied.

My roommate's English communication skills have improved over the months since our first meeting. To my chagrin, she had ceased using the Machine, insisting on "full immersion" whenever she was at the hostel. She was still not fully at ease with the language, of course. Or with me for that matter. Kimi's eyes darted back and forth, as if looking for something in the room to beat me over the head with. Meanwhile, I cupped her face with my hands.

"Don't you get what this means?I whispered. "Psychopaths are incapable of love. But I was in love before. That means I'm absolutely not a psychopath." I paused for emphasis. "It's a big deal."

Kimi gulped hard and nodded. "That sounds nice," she repeated. Then she went to the back of her closet, where she preferred to go when she felt "overwhelmed."

"David," I repeated after she had vanished behind many winter coats, "is all the proof I need."

This discovery gave me hope. The fact that I had been in love before demonstrated my ability to acquire social feelings. The romance may have been brief, but it had happened. The emotions had been real. They still were. Despite the distance and time that had passed, my feelings for David had not faded. I enjoyed thinking about him. I liked talking with him. It helped me feel normal. Which is why I never lost contact with him.

The first time I phoned, it was on a whim—a quick talk a few months after summer camp to see what he was up to. I assumed we would only converse for a few minutes. But we did not. The first phone call lasted hours. Following that, we talked all the time. David was the only person in the world with whom I felt both honest and safe. For me, this was a desirable dynamic. It reminded me of my early years in San Francisco, when I used to sit beneath the table and joyously confess secrets to my mother. That form of safety has long been abandoned, with good reason, in favor of the security provided by deception. But what I got in security came at the expense of companionship. It was alienating. And a part of me desired to be seen, to feel comfortable through the lens of authenticity. That's why I like conversing with David. I've never lied to him.

"Guess what," I said later that night. "I am not a psychopath!""

He laughed. "Are you certain about that?"" he stated. "Let me talk to Kimi."

"Stop," I instructed. "This is important," I told him, detailing my most recent insight.

"I'm confused," he conceded once I was finished. "If sociopaths and psychopaths are so different, why are they often grouped together?"

I had the exact same question. And the answer, I reasoned after a few more excursions to the library, was (one again) due to the literature. The basic works on sociopathy and psychopathy did not always make clear differences. One book would say that the two were identical. Another would claim they were distinct. There was no consistency. When slang-appropriation corrupted the titles of mental conditions, the field of psychology changed them. To reduce the stigma associated with these terms, "mental retardation" and "multiple personality disorder" were substituted with "intellectual disability" and "dissociative identity disorder," respectively. The problem is that, while well-intentioned, altering vocabulary to reflect current events significantly hampers scientific inquiry on these topics.

The term "sociopath" was introduced in 1930 by psychologist G. E. Partridge defined the condition as a pathology characterized by a lack of behavioral conformity to prosocial principles. In other words, these are people who do not engage in ways that benefit society and instead purposefully cause friction. Sociopathy was later added to the first edition of the DSM in 1952. However, once the fifth edition of Cleckley's The Mask of Sanity was published (and popularized) in 1976, the term "psychopath" came to refer to both diseases. However, because there was no formal change of guard about the nomenclature, academics and doctors continued to use "psychopath" and "sociopath" synonymously. This resulted in a considerable deal of dispute over diagnostic criteria and overall knowledge.

That summer, I sat at my workstation at Dad's house, reeling from figures discovered during another library visit. Despite the debate over the disorder's name, researchers appeared to concur on its prevalence. According to various studies, sociopaths make up almost 5% of the population, which is roughly equal to the number of people who have panic disorder. It seemed absurd that a condition affecting millions of people was not given more attention by the psychological association, especially since the major trait of sociopathy is indifference, and the principal consequence of unrelenting apathy is destructive activity. I pondered what these folks were doing to keep themselves in check.

It was a question I longed to answer for myself. In the months since school ended, I'd been trying to find new ways to cope with my growing restlessness. With just so much time I could spend at the library and no constant stream of fraternity parties and stolen cars to startle me into action, I had to resort to other techniques of apathy reduction. Fortunately, the City of Angels offered many opportunities.

I discovered that breaking into residences was much like riding a bike. I hadn't done it since high school, but it felt familiar and effective. I felt less restless while lounging in strangers' homes while they worked. I felt calm. But without my mother's real estate lockbox code, getting into properties was much more difficult than it had been when I was younger. I spent countless hours monitoring residents to determine when they were typically out of the house and for how long. I went to great lengths to go inside homes without calling attention to my entry points. I became excellent at picking locks and created my own set of equipment.

I sat on Dad's living room couch one afternoon, holding a collection of ancient padlocks and a tension wrench in my lap. I'd taught myself how to pick locks years ago but had only just begun to practice really. The workout was cathartic. In many respects, manipulating a lock was similar to searching for my own apathetic pressure valve. I enjoyed working it out.

I just need to find the appropriate balance of conduct and distraction, I reasoned as I worked on a difficult antique padlock, and I'll be able to find my equilibrium.

I closed my eyes and felt my way around the interior of the lock. Moving the hook through the cylinder, I pressed on the pins. I felt the tension wrench give slightly against my thumb. "Almost there," I muttered. After some moderate pushing, I could feel the final pin release when I pushed it above the shear line. The lock made a satisfying pop when the shank snapped open. "Gotcha." I opened my eyes and smiled at my accomplishment. I wondered if I should be a locksmith. Then, for reasons I can't understand, an even better notion occurred to me.

I wonder if I should be a babysitter.

Working as a childcare provider may have appeared like an unusual decision for someone who had recently discovered she was a psychopath. But, I reasoned, children were less likely to notice that I was not normal. They were less inclined to call me out for refusing to play by the rules. Kids would forgive my sins if I was entertaining and innovative. I thought it was a creative method to keep myself entertained.

Granted, I was not what one might call a "kid" person. I wasn't bubbly, expressive, affectionate, or anything else you'd expect from a traditional nanny. Surprisingly, I was hired very quickly by a well-known actor in the upscale Los Angeles neighborhood of Brentwood. Perhaps more surprising, I enjoyed the job. The three children I was tasked with managing, with their distinctive personalities and charming temperaments, were like delightful interactive puzzles. I appreciated learning about their different personalities. In my own way, I adored them. My strong sympathies for those children and instinct to defend them at all costs gave me a new sense of hope. Perhaps I wasn't such a hopeless case after all.

My dark cravings were easier to control as the months passed and I settled into my new position. My leisure time was limited, so I had less opportunity to get into trouble. I understood that merely distracting myself was not a foolproof solution to the destructive inclinations, but at the time, I was thankful for whatever assistance I could get.

My internal climate resembled a balloon. Things that kept me busy, such as school and work, were my helium, propelling the balloon above its apathetic baseline. However, it was not permanent. When I wasn't distracted by a responsibility or coasting off the consequences of bad behavior, I got listless. The balloon would lose its buoyancy, and I would soon begin looking for ways to jolt myself into emotion.

"If this pressure is caused by the brain's subconscious desire to jolt itself out of apathy," I reasoned, "then stuck stress must be an anxious reaction to apathy." Based on my experience, this made sense. For the majority of my life, I was surrounded by "normal" people, therefore I was constantly trying to hide what made me different. It was the only way I knew to stay under the radar and be secure. That is why, at the first sign of pressure—or mounting apathy—I would become concerned. Knowing that the pressure would eventually force my hand, and that the only way to get rid of it was to do something horrible, I began to feel helpless. I would begin to feel confined.

Unless I was alone, I realized with surprise.

Indeed, my reaction to apathy was not always uncomfortable. Often, I'd relished the experience. For example, the time I walked home from the slumber party and climbed into that automobile; the hours spent at the abandoned house near Grandma's; the covert outings to the cellar at the Rockefeller estate; and the late-night drives in stolen vehicles. All of those times, I was consumed by apathy, yet I wasn't disturbed at all. Quite the contrary. I felt free.

I concluded since no one was watching me. Without the need to justify my lack of emotion, I could simply enjoy it.

This was a revelation, and as I left the library that day, another realization occurred to me.

If I knew that trapped tension was caused by my situational discomfort with indifference, I reasoned, why not take a more proactive approach to alleviating it? In other words, if my anxiety is prompted by my discomfort with apathy, it may be possible to reduce that anxiety (and the harmful behavior that frequently results) by learning how to accept the indifference so that it no longer causes me distress.

The hypothesis was made logical. Even though I had a better grasp of what was causing the pressure and why there was so much stress associated with it, I still didn't know how to remove it. I also didn't comprehend under what conditions I would or wouldn't become nervous about being apathetic. Sometimes my apathy made me uneasy. Sometimes it did not.

But the basic line was this: In order to continue to be an active (although covertly broken) member of society and enjoy all of the benefits of membership, I needed to change my fearful response. I'd have to accept my apathetic nature rather than be afraid of it. The longer I let my apathy develop, the longer I waited to get my "fix" of sensation, the more likely I was to get worried and lose control of my reaction. So, why wait? I asked myself. Wouldn't it make more sense to participate in smaller acts of "bad" behavior more frequently, rather than larger actions less frequently? I decided to test my theory.

The next morning, I awoke earlier than usual. I got myself a cup of coffee, sat on the window bench in the living room, and stared across the street. The individuals who lived there, a young couple from Tarzana, were Warner Brothers executives. They had been married for a year and spent their honeymoon in Cabo. I didn't come upon this information by chance. I got it by chatting them up at a Fourth of July block party that summer. I also knew they'd installed a state-of-the-art alarm system, but only used it when they went "on vacation." They also owned a dog named Samson, who "only looked mean." Most crucially, I knew they were always at work by 8:15.

I sat comfortably in my perch and watched them exit the front door and make their way to matching SUVs parked in the driveway. After they left—right on time—I went to my bedroom and dressed.

Ten minutes later, I stood at their rear door. The deadbolt was old, but a well-known brand. I quickly unlocked it with my tools and stepped inside. When I stepped into the kitchen, the silence entranced me for a brief minute.

A structure that has just been broken into has a unique silence. It's almost as if the house can't believe what has happened and gulped, sucking up all the air with it. There is incredible peace. I could spend an eternity in the silence, utterly absorbed in the current moment and at peace.

My moment was interrupted by the tap of canine paws running down the corridor. "Hey, buddy," I murmured, kneeling to hand Samson a handful of dog biscuits. "Do you mind if I hang out here for a bit?"Samson didn't mind. He definitely appreciated his company. We strolled through the home together. I surveyed the trinkets on the tables and the photographs on the walls. I looked through the books on the shelves and examined the clothes in the closets. I took nothing. I caused no disturbance. I simply existed in a world where I wasn't supposed to be.

Samson moaned and pressed against my legs as I attempted to leave. I gave him one more squeeze, silently closed the door behind me, and stepped into the backyard, amazed by the change in atmosphere. Even though I'd barely been inside the house for a half hour, everything felt different. The air was sweeter. The world is less frenetic. I exhaled with relief and headed back to my house.

My disinterest was like a dragon that needed feeding. If I ignored it, it would consume me. So I set it on a diet. I did exactly what was required to give myself the essential "jolts" of emotion. I never pursued it further—even when I was tempted, which was frequently. I planned out my misbehavior as if it were a doctor's prescription. And I never missed a dose.

CHAPTER 8

BORDERLINE

A cottage sits just off Mulholland Drive, on the route to my father's Beverly Hills home. Unlike the magnificent mansions that line the renowned avenue, this house is modest and dilapidated. During visits to Dad's, I'd slow down to catch a sight of the little elderly lady who was almost always outdoors tending her rose gardens. She was rarely alone. An elderly man, whom I believed was her husband, would generally sit in a lawn chair nearby, watching her work while reading. He balanced a coffee cup on a stack of books in the grass beside him.

"I'm going to buy that house someday," I said.

A few months later, I was sitting at an office on San Vicente Boulevard. The afternoon light had begun to set below the horizon, and if I tilted my head properly, I could just make out the arc of the ocean through the window.

"You're changing the subject again, Patric," Dr. Carlin commented.

At my father's suggestion, I began visiting a therapist. Dr. Carlin, a psychologist, came highly recommended. After hearing my history and stories about my spells of apathy and destructive behavior, she felt I had sociopathic personality disorder. So she requested that the PCL test, sometimes known as the psychopathy checklist, be administered.

I squinted out the window. "That's because your subjects are so annoying," I replied.

"I think it's a good idea," she softly said.

My therapist's observation that I was an empathy-seeking psychopath was insightful, although not unexpected. In many ways, I was like the lost duckling from the children's book. Are you my mother? Except, instead of a brave tiny bird with a loving heart and identity concerns looking for its mother, I was an antisocial outlier with a narrow emotional range and a tendency of lying in need of a friend. Despite my diagnosis, I wasn't any closer to understanding why I was the way I was.

I didn't have much time to think about it. After a brief post-graduation break, I accepted my father's offer and joined his new company. During my first few months on the job, I shadowed him and several of his associates, making it my mission to study every facet of music management. What I discovered was surprising. I rapidly recognized that the music industry was a sleight-of-hand macrocosm in which I excelled. Few people noticed the mysterious forces hiding behind the scenes, distracted by the draw of the music and the performers' carefully created mystique. However, this was where the true magic was taking place. Dark magic.

From backroom payola transactions and side-hustling A&R scouts to murky producer agreements and double-dipping management firms, the music industry was "a cruel and shallow money trench, a long plastic hallway where thieves and pimps run free." At least Hunter S. Thompson seemed to believe so. It was difficult to argue.

My psychological horizons broadened as soon as I started working as a talent manager. Suddenly, I didn't feel like the only sociopath in the world. Not only did the majority of the people I encountered appear to appreciate my personality type, but many seemed eager to adopt it. Indeed, I was surprised by the amount of people in the entertainment industry who, after hearing about my disease, expressed a similar attitude.

"Oh, I'm totally a sociopath," Nathan, a music producer, admitted shortly after we met. "I don't give a fuck about anything."

One look over his production contract revealed that this was not totally truthful. Nathan appeared to be very concerned about royalties—to the point that any artist contracted with his production firm had to give up practically all of their creative ownership.

"But it probably explains why I do so well at my job. "I like to do bad things," he said with a mischievous grin. "I like being a sociopath."

Prior to entering the music profession, I struggled to find people who would accept me for who I am, let alone acknowledge having a similar personality type. But now I was encircled! The result was hypnotizing (and initially blinding). I was so intrigued by the promise of a like-minded company that I paid little attention to the credibility of my supposed cohorts' sociopathic self-diagnoses. Like a dehydrated traveler, I drank every last drop. At least I did at first. And then I met Jennifer.

Jennifer was a record label executive in charge of the sophomore album release of one of my father's most valuable customers. Dad encouraged us to meet to ensure the success of the new record.

"The rock world is nothing like the pop world," she told me one night. It was a year after I began working as a manager, and we were drinking at Casa Vega, my favorite Mexican restaurant in the Valley. "You've gotta be tough to survive," she told me, "especially if you're a girl."

I smiled and stepped rapidly into the opening she had unintentionally created. "Well, that's perfect for me because I'm a sociopath."

She grinned, assuming I was joking, but then listened intently as I briefed her on my background and diagnosis.

"Whoa," she said after I finished. "That's amazing." She lowered her voice and leaned in, conspiratorially. "To be honest, I've always sort of wondered if I was a sociopath."

"Huh," I responded. I've been hearing that a lot recently.

"No, but you know what I mean?" Jennifer pressed. "The things that make other people cry do not make me cry. Like true crime stories. "I am obsessed with it!" She looked around again. "And I have totally fantasized about killing people."

I shake my head. "So, that's... "Wanting to kill someone does not automatically make you a sociopath," I explained. "That is something of a misconception. Sociopathy is widely misunderstood—"

"No, but you know what I mean?" Jennifer repeated, cutting me off. "I love dark stuff, like vampires." She smiled. "It's probably why I got into marketing for rock bands!"

I was beginning to wonder if I should reconsider my policy of revealing my personality type. But I hardly had time to think about it before she placed a hand on my forearm. "I get you, girl," she said, nodding.

I looked down at Jennifer's hand and noticed her baby finger was covered in surgical bandages. "What happened there?" I inquired, pleased to change the subject.

Jennifer jerked her hand away. "Oooooh," she exclaimed. "I rescued a pit bull. She's the sweetest thing, but last month she got into a battle with my other dog. I tried to separate them, and she bit my finger off."

This horrible disclosure caused me to choke on my cocktail. I coughed and took a large sip. "I'm sorry," I replied. "She bit your finger off?"

Jennifer nodded. "Yeah. My neighbor had to drive me to the ER. Fortunately, physicians were able to sew it back on." She smiled.

"Do you have any doggies?"

I was speechless. "Uhm, no, I don't have—hold on a sec," I answered, attempting to gather my thoughts. "What happened to… your other dog?" I pestered you.

Jennifer grimaced. "Yes, that is a continuous concern. Lady is only violent against other dogs, so I have to keep them apart all the time." She paused to ask our waiter for more drinks. "Dogs are the best." Especially now that I am divorced. "Did you know I am divorced?"

I shake my head. Jennifer didn't appear to notice.

"I was married for ten years and all I have to show for it is this dingy little house in the Valley. Next time, I want someone to look after me, you know? "Like a rich guy." Jennifer downed the remainder of her margarita. "That's what I have now—a wealthy man. "His name is Joel, and he's extremely wealthy." Her eyes expanded. "He knows other rich folks, you know. We could set you up, and we could have double dates!"

I shake my head. "I'm not really—"

"He's got this huge place in Beverly Hills flats," she added wistfully. "I feel, like, that's where I should live, too, y'know?" Her gaze darkened slightly as she peered into space before adding, "I deserve it."

I was perplexed. Without understanding what else to do, I began modeling her actions. I put on my most compassionate expression and lay my hand against her forearm, taking care not to disturb her reattached finger. "I get you, girl," I said.

But I did not get her. And the more I learned about her, the more puzzled I grew. Jennifer's speculation that she was a psychopath nearly made sense, as did many of the self-diagnostic "confessions" I'd been hearing from folks in the entertainment industry. She frequently complained of feeling "empty." She was impetuous and destructive, just like me. She was also quite insensitive, exhibiting either impunity or disregard for other people's boundaries. However, I immediately learned that this was the extent of the parallels.

Jennifer appeared to have an abundance of feelings, but I lacked them. For starters, she had extreme mood swings. She'd go from pleasure to agitation for no obvious reason. She also had a bad temper and little self-control, frequently storming out of meetings or yelling at coworkers when she didn't get her way. But, maybe most unlike me, Jennifer appeared to be extremely unstable. This was especially true for her romantic relationships. Even the tiniest apparent rejection would throw her into a cognitive dissonance state.

"Patric!" Jennifer shouted. "I have got to talk to you!"

It was the morning of the album's release, a month after our initial encounter at Casa Vega, and I'd just arrived at a radio station where she had scheduled a live interview with the band. My shoulders slumped as I stepped out of my car and saw her waiting for me in the parking lot. Ugh, I thought. I could tell she was upset and untidy.

"Why haven't you returned my calls?" she asked urgently, gasping for air as she trotted across the lot. "Something really bad happened, and I need to talk to you," Jennifer insisted.

I shake my head. "There is no chance. "The interview is in ten minutes."

"You do not comprehend. It's important!" Jennifer put her hand on my arm and softly drew me closer. "You know my dog Lady?"

I sighed anxiously as I watched the lead vocalist approach the radio station's foyer. "Are you serious?" "I am not listening to a dog story right now."

"She killed my neighbor's dog!"

I was shocked. "What?"

"You realize I have to keep her away from my other dog, right? So I have started placing her in the backyard. My neighbors keep their dog in the backyard. Anyway, Lady must have dug under the fence or something because she grabbed their dog and killed him! "I saw everything happen."

Now it was my turn to take her arm. Jennifer's elbow produced a pleasant snap as I hauled her out of my clients' sight. "You watched your dog dig under a fence, attack another dog, and kill it?" I demanded.

She nodded.

"Why?" I questioned. "How come you didn't stop her? Why didn't you do anything?

In answer, she faintly displayed her recently reattached finger.

"Oh, you've gotta be fucking kidding me," I said, truly disgusted. "What did your neighbor say?"

"That's the thing," Jennifer remarked, her voice increasing with alarm. "After Lady was, like, done, I freaked. I knew I needed to hide the body, so I brought it out onto the street and left it there. They'll blame themselves if the information gets out, right? "They'll think it was hit by a car?"

"What?!" I exclaimed. "What the fuck is wrong with you?"

"I had no choice!" Jennifer shrieked and began to cry. "Last time, she took me to the hospital. She knows Lady is aggressive! If she finds out, she'll have me take her down!"

"Oh my God," I said as I realized the link. "Is this the same neighbor who drove you to the ER?" "What the hell is wrong with you?" I asked again.

"I told you," Jennifer emphasized. "I'm a sociopath!"

"You're not a sociopath," I exclaimed, enraged. "You're a fucking moron."

She wailed, and her wails drew attention in the parking lot. "Oh my God, what if I get caught?" She groaned again. "I feel so bad," she said through tears. Grabbing my wrists, she cried, "Patric!" You have to help me! You need to tell me what to do!"

I freed myself from her grip. "You want my advice?" I hissed. "Go home." Clean yourself up and stop spinning out. I will tackle the fucking interview on my own."

That seems to jolt her out of her mania. "Yes," she replied, sniffling. "You're correct. "I should just take a deep breath and be nice to myself." She exaggerated her inhalation and exhalation before saying, "I'm not going home, though."

"Why not?" I inquired, immediately regretting the inquiry.

"The guy I'm seeing, Joel," she said. "I'll just go to his house. After a long week, I deserve some shopping therapy!"

I actively resisted the urge to stab her with my keys. My nails were sharp and punctured the flesh of my palms. "Fine," I replied calmly. "I do not care. "Just get it together."

I turned toward the station, but Jennifer wasn't finished.

"Patric? "May I ask you something?" Tears and hysteria had subsided.

I spun around. "What?"

"So Joel offered me one of his cars to drive, correct? It's nice. It's a Porsche. But he didn't hand me his credit card or anything. I kind of think that's dickish." She paused. "That was dickish, right?" she repeated. "Like, we've been seeing each other for a long time, and I'm always at his apartment. I feel like he should have given me his shopping card."

I took a minute to truly embrace my loathing. "Totally," I finally said. Then I entered the station.

I arrived in time for the interview. After directing the band to the DJ booth, I grabbed a seat in the listening section. Fortunately, the room was vacant, and as I stared into space, I could feel apathy slowly rising. But I couldn't relax for very long. Something was bothering me, a feeling of unease. I looked down at my hands. My palms were bleeding.

CHAPTER 9

HOME

I was at home late one evening a few weeks later when I was startled by a knock on the door. I got up from the couch and looked through the peephole. My mouth fell as I flung open the door.

David smiled uneasily. "I wasn't sure if you were serious," he replied, "but I figured I'd roll the dice."

I jumped into his arms and nearly knocked him over.

"How'd you get here?" I eventually asked, my voice muffled by his neck.

He laughed. "I drove, foolishly. I packed up everything I owned and just went west."

I drew back and glanced at him, still shocked. "For me?"

"For you," he stated. Then he kissed me.

It was just how I'd imagined it would be in the few instances when I allowed myself to dream. In an instant, all my old emotions returned, splintering my apathy as they soared. David's strong arms and stable demeanor seemed like what I'd always imagined "home" to be.

There was no unpleasant transition time. It felt as if we had never been separated. Overnight, I moved from being a self-sufficient single woman to half of a pair. I will confess that the transition was abrupt. I'd never been in a traditional relationship as an adult, and I'd never been the type of person to jump into anything. I preferred seclusion. Secrecy. Discipline. I preferred to keep people at arms' length and my home spotless. So I astonished myself when, from the minute David arrived unannounced on my doorstep, I gave up everything to be with him.

"You're like a magician," he explained.

The following weekend, we relaxed in the Los Angeles sunshine while sipping wine at Moraga Vineyards. The private winery was hidden behind a strong fence in a gorge of the Santa Monica Mountains, and it was one of my favorite spots in the city. I'd been asked to taste a few months ago and was overjoyed that David could finally accompany me. "This place," he added, glancing around. "It is like a mirage. "How did you even find it?"

He was correct. Moraga was like a mirage. A lovely vineyard buried in the middle of Bel Air, I had no idea it existed until I discovered it on a walk one day. Astonished by the seemingly endless rows of beautiful grapevines, I made my way to the street and searched around before finding the entrance. Then I knocked on the door and introduced myself to the homeowners.

"So you just knocked on the door?" "David asked." "What did you say?"

"The truth!" I responded. "That this place is the Mecca of secret gardens and they deserve a medal for turning the land into a working vineyard."

"Wait," David interrupted. "Who is 'they'?"

The owners. "Tom and Ruth Jones."

"Hold up," he exclaimed, his eyes wide. "Is this Tom Jones' house?" "The Tom Jones?"

"No," I replied, chuckling. "Well, yes, this is Tom Jones' house. But not the singer. Trust me, though: This Tom Jones is the best Tom Jones."

"So, you just walked up to the door and said, 'Hi.'" David shakes his head. "Did they freak out?"

"No!" I replied. "They were really nice and informed me all about the property and its history. Then they asked for my address so they could put me on the list for tastings and whatnot." I waved my hand around, taking in the surroundings. "And voilà!"

"Like I said," he murmured, his eyes gleaming. "You're a magician."

I felt the same way about him. Suddenly, I was no longer burdened by the duty of controlling my apathy. When David arrived, it vanished, replaced by tremendous sensations of love. Mad, frantic, all-consuming love that never seemed to end. I no longer had to be concerned about medications, cheating strategies, pressure, or psychopathic anxiousness. I could just be. With nothing to hold me back, I began exploring life as a "normal" person.

It reminded me of Super Toy Run, a show I used to watch on Nickelodeon. During the show, children were allowed five minutes to sprint through a Toys "R" Us and collect anything they could. As a child, I spent hours imagining the situation, categorizing the aisles, and honing my own method for getting the best results in the least amount of time. And now I'm doing something similar. My objective was simple: run around life and get as many typical experiences as possible. Going to dinner and a movie after work was a treat. A Sunday morning stroll through the neighborhood, sipping coffee and holding hands, was an adventure. The more ordinary, the better. I seized every opportunity to be conventional. Ordinary things, like going grocery shopping or snuggling into bed with him at the end of the day, made me happy. For the first time in my life, I wasn't merely dreaming about a life devoid of emotional detachment and shadow-self temptations. I was experiencing it. I was free! I wanted to proclaim my excitement from the rooftops.

And I wasn't the only one thankful for David's influence. My father, who was startled by the speed of our connection, welcomed the shift in his daughter's lifestyle.

"You really seem to like this guy," he joked.

Dad and I were having our weekly Sunday dinner at The Palm. As usual, we gathered at the bar while waiting for our table. David had rapidly become a regular at our "family" dinners, although he was running a little late. I was overjoyed at the opportunity to gush behind his back.

"Dad," I admitted, "I don't simply like him. I'm like an insane person. I am insanely, madly in love with him!" The waiter placed a frozen martini in front of me, and I took a big swallow, slurping up the thin chips of ice floating on top. "He makes me believe that all of my flaws aren't really flaws, but rather misinterpreted. I feel like the best version of myself when I'm with him. I am serious; if he asked me to marry him tomorrow, I would.

"Whoa," Dad responded. "Maybe pump the brakes a bit."

"Why?" I questioned. "David is the guy." "I know it in my soul." I stopped and then lowered my voice. "It might sound nuts," I responded, "but it's like I found my missing half—my good half." I shook my head in astonishment as I pondered this. "All the things I've always struggled with, empathy, emotions." I paused again. "It's as if David has filled the space in my heart where those things should be. "And he's a wonderful person, Dad." I exhaled. "He motivates me to be better. "He makes me believe that I, too, can be a good person."

This was true. David was patient. Thoughtful. Calm. But, unlike my sense of peace (which was frequently just apathy), David exuded a serene quiet. This was visible not only in his manner, but also in his extraordinary capacity to see the sublime in the ordinary. Whether it was taking the time to intentionally enjoy the perfect sandwich from Bay Cities Deli or pausing to point out a constellation in the night sky, David was an expert at relishing simplicity. Surprisingly, for the first time in my life, I was able to join in. Even household chores, such as cooking, now bring me immense joy.

Though I had always liked food, I had never been particularly interested in learning how to prepare it myself. But once David arrived, cooking became my love. I accepted the role of happy housewife and began preparing our meals almost every night. I started with the basics and gradually became more experimental, spending hours planning menus and experimenting with different flavor profiles. After work, I would go immediately to the kitchen to chop the items and choose the wine. Once the supper was prepared, I'd take layers of cakes from the refrigerator (where I'd left them to chill after baking them in the morning) and sit at the dining room table. There, I'd slice each layer in two with thread, exactly as my mother had done, and spread homemade icing between them, piling the pieces into decadent towers.

Sitting there, eating chocolate off my fingertips, I kept thinking about the man and the German shepherd I had followed home to his wonderful little family. The slice of life I'd photographed through their living room window stayed crystal vivid, like an antique Polaroid stuck for years to a dusty corner of a vision board. I imagined that one day I will be exactly like them. And here I was.

Leaning hard into my vision of domestic bliss, I always made sure the house was spotless before David arrived home. After supper was prepared, I would carefully set the table, light candles, and walk around the home to ensure that everything was neat and tidy. However, all of these duties were pleasure-delaying strategies that set the atmosphere for my favorite ritual: choosing the evening's soundtrack.

I stored the records in the living room, on a bookcase next to the fireplace. There were hundreds of LPs, the majority of which belonged to my father, who had spent his entire life in radio. But now, I've started making my own contributions. Jackie McLean, John Coltrane, Hank Mobley, Thelonious Monk, B.B. King, McCoy Tyner, Bill Evans, Duke Ellington, and Nina Simone were among the most recent additions to my collection. I'd kept the albums for years but hadn't put them on display. I had kept them secret for a specific reason.

Jazz music has always had a strong, almost supernatural impact on me. The rhapsodic melodies never lifted my spirits, but they did sit alongside them, like a silent friend or a wonderfully suited glass of wine. I was always cautious with the dosage. I believe I was scared that if I listened too much, the song might lose its power. Or perhaps I'd begin to identify it with a specific memory or period. I wanted to keep it pure and potent, so I avoided any chance of overindulgence. Instead, I would wait until the pressure became unbearable before reaching for my CDs. With jazz playing in my headphones, I felt less alone and more accepting of the nothingness within. I never had to change the lyrics to fit my absence. I never had to do anything except listen. In this manner, the music was its own reward, and I cherished the chance to escape within it.

Living with David, however, I had no need for such restraint. Whether it was jazz, food, wine, or sex, I could have it all whenever I wanted. I didn't always have to be in control. I didn't need to be measured. I knew I was safe with him, therefore I was free. I was free to be normal. I was free to prepare my meals, drink my wine, and seduce my man. I was free to listen to my music every night.

To be honest, I always made a point of doing so before David arrived home. Even though our musical interests were nearly identical in every other way, David detested jazz and made no secret of it. "This music sounds insane!" he exclaimed one night, chuckling. "It makes no sense!" I laughed with him.

David worked in technology and preferred linear systems. His dedication to rationality was unwavering. He believed that there was just one "right" way to accomplish things. It's one of the reasons he became such an accomplished computer programmer. He never made a mistake. Ever. He was thorough, patient, and did not cut corners. That's why it came as no surprise when, shortly after relocating to Los Angeles, he was employed by an internet marketing start-up to oversee the development of all of their digital projects. He obtained the job with little effort, and we sank even deeper into our happy household life.

CHAPTER 10

LIBERTY

It had occurred to me several weeks prior. I'd been sitting close to the picture window in the living room, listening to music while waiting for David to arrive home. It was the same window through which I'd frequently watched the Tarzana neighbors, ensuring they'd both departed for work before entering their home for my weekly "prescription." I observed the dark, deserted house across the street. The couple had relocated, and the property was for sale. Would it feel the same? I wondered.

I didn't bother closing the door behind me as I went. Miles Davis' Volume 2 played from my living room, his trumpet wafting into my ears as I walked. I tapped my lock pick kit against my thigh. The metal tools clinked satisfyingly in my pocket. I'd never been to the house after dark, and the yard felt strangely alien as I neared the back door. I turned the knob and noticed that it was unlocked. "So not technically breaking and entering," I said quietly.

When I stepped into the kitchen, my muscle memory kicked in, and I readied myself to meet my canine accomplice. But Samson was long gone. The moonlight poured through the windows, providing just enough illumination to help me navigate the unoccupied house. I entered the living room and climbed the stairs to the second floor, running my hand along the blank walls as I went. Then I went down the small hallway into what had been the main bedroom. From the window, I could see my own house across the road. If anyone saw me up here, I assumed they'd think I was a ghost. Seen yet unseen. The finest of both worlds.

I placed my hands on the window frame and pressed my thumbs on the latches to gently lift the pane. Canyon breezes invaded the room, accompanied by the notes of woodwinds still playing from my living room speakers. I felt everything and nothing at once. The sensation was narcotic, and I slid down the wall, stopping beneath the open window. I laid my head against the ledge.

"If this isn't heaven," I said, "I don't know what is." I grinned as I stared at the shadows on the opposite wall. Being inside the house seemed different in some way, and it wasn't just because there was less furniture. I felt different. Something had changed, and I loved it, but I couldn't pinpoint exactly what.

I remembered a favorite Radiohead tune. "For a moment there," I sang gently, "I found myself." It was a verse from "Karma Police," slightly tweaked to fit my situation. As I sang, my mind turned to Dad's comment about becoming a sociopathic Buddhist. I peered around the empty room, amused. "How much karma would a visit like this cost?" It was a rhetorical question, but it made me think.

Being in this house does not harm anyone. And it doesn't feel "bad," I reflected. So, who's to say it is? It was the same question I'd asked myself back in middle school. After all these years, I still didn't have an answer.

"Only now I don't care," I said quietly.

I turned my head to the side, and a glint of metal caught my eye in the corner of the room. I crept across the floor to explore. It was, or had been, a keychain featuring the Statue of Liberty. The chain was damaged, and the keyring was missing.

I lifted up the statue and stroked my thumb around its smooth base. "You're coming with me," I assured her. Then I sat for a time in pleasant stillness. A burst of headlights on the street below jolted me out of my trance. I stood and took a deep, pleasant inhale. Then I closed the bedroom window, descended the stairs, and left the house. Only this time, I did not bother with the back entry. I walked out the front door, the suggestive music from my living room still mild and distant, but rising louder as it welcomed me home.

In bed that night, I informed David about my visit to the house across the street and showed him the treasure I discovered there.

"I think it should be our signal," I stated.

"What do you mean?" he inquired.

"When I do something unconventional, I'll leave it on the table next to the front door," I told him, selecting my words carefully. "That way, you'll know."

David drew me close and asked, "'Unorthodox'?" "Is that what we're calling it?" I giggled.

"Yeah," I replied. "So, this is our unconventional statue. "It's just like the Bat Signal."

He shakes his head. "It's nothing like the Bat-Signal."

I made a show of rolling my eyes. "Whatever. The objective is that when you see it, you can ask me what I did, and you can count on me to be truthful. If you don't want to know, I will not tell you. "Whatever you want."

"What I want," David answered, "is to understand why you went over there." He sounded dissatisfied. "You mentioned you haven't felt like doing anything awful recently. You mentioned you hadn't felt the apathy since I arrived."

"I was getting to that," I answered, eager to clarify. "Because you're correct." Tonight, I was not apathetic at all. "I went because I wanted to," I informed him. "Isn't it wild?"

"Wild how?" He twisted, dug his elbow into the pillow, and rested his head on his hand. "That's the part I don't understand. You stated that you disliked feeling obligated to do such things and were relieved to be able to be normal again. You've been telling me that was your wish almost since the day we met.

"Yes! And that is true!" I squeezed his arm warmly. "That's what's so crazy about it." I motioned around the house. "We do everything together throughout our lives. It has been fantastic. "Living like this with you, feeling like..." I began laughing. "That's it—just feeling. Consistent feeling. "God, David," I said. "You can't imagine what it's like."

"Then why?" he inquired gently. "I guarantee I am not judging you. I am just wondering. If you only feel the need to break the rules when you don't feel, then why—if you've been having so much 'feeling' with me—did you break into that house tonight?"

"Because I didn't feel like I had to," I explained. "I thought I wanted to. I wasn't pursuing an emotion, attempting to get ahead of my disinterest, or keeping the pot from boiling over. And, as you mentioned, I knew you wouldn't judge me.

I got up and sat cross-legged on the bed, my heart racing with excitement. "It's like without the anxiety of being 'outed,' there's me the sociopath," I said, extending one palm to the side. "But now there's also me, the normal person." I repeated the action with the opposing hand. "It's like I discovered a missing piece or something. "And now, boom!" I clapped my hands together.

"Boom what?" he inquired.

I groaned and shook my head. "That's the thing," I said. "I haven't worked that part out yet." David collapsed to his back, shaking his head at the ceiling.

"All I know is that tonight, in that house, I felt the same way I had in elementary school when I stabbed Syd. And then I locked the girls in the restroom." I chose not to tell him about the cat in Virginia.

David appeared extremely troubled. "But how is that good?" he inquired.

He listened intently as I described the euphoric effect that violent acts had always had and my unwavering unwillingness to commit them as a result. "I've never found anything else that produces that same feeling." I halted. "Until tonight."

"So, what is that feeling?" David asked while sitting up. "Can you describe it to me?"

As I considered how to describe it, my sight slipped into the folds of the large white bedspread. "Surrender," I said gently. "Complete, apathetic capitulation. I don't care about anything, and more importantly, I don't care about not caring. And I have perfect control.

"I still don't get how that's good," David said.

"It's fantastic since so much of my negative behavior has sprung from fear and concern about not feeling. But none of that came into play tonight." I grinned just thinking about it. "I did something terrible tonight just because I wanted to. I did it because I could, not because I was under pressure or stressed out. I knew I wouldn't feel regret, fear, remorse, or anything." I shrugged and then smiled. "I enjoyed being myself because I knew it would be fun," I explained. "And when I did, I had that ecstatic feeling. A sense of wholeness. "Total exposure without any stress." I let out a contented exhalation. "It was a sense of 'this is me, this is who I am.' And I don't care who knows it or what anyone thinks of it; I don't feel horrible about it." I could tell he was still trying to understand. "I promise, it was a nice feeling."

"Okay," he said. "Look. In the big scheme of things, what you did tonight was not particularly horrible. I got it. Technically, you should not have been there, but whatever. My only concern is a complete lack of guilt. It's no big deal to not feel awful about walking into an empty house. The issue arises when one does not feel awful about larger issues. I'm worried about it becoming a slippery slope for you."

I began to argue, but he interrupted me, adding, "I know you think it's pointless, honey, but it isn't. Guilt is one of the things that binds people together, you know. Society would collapse if no one felt awful about doing bad things." He hesitated and then, "Guilt, for lack of a better word, is good."

"So you're Reverse Gordon Gekko," I remarked.

David laughed. "What do you expect after twelve years of Catholic school?"

I gave him a sneaky smile. "Well, maybe I could help you shed some of that schoolboy guilt," I suggested, sliding upon him. I laid my lips on his ear. "Sociopathy has its perks, you know," I said quietly. "Your first lesson could start next door… with me."

"You wanna go over there now?"

"Why not?" "There's definitely nobody home..."

David grabbed my waist, flipped me over, and pinned me to the bed. Then he kissed me, and we forgot about our neighbors' house.

The next morning, I tossed the small statue into the drawer of my bedside table. I didn't anticipate utilizing it anytime soon. Despite my trip across the street, I was no longer interested in exploring prospects for misadventure. But it turned out that I didn't need to look. Opportunities came to me.

CHAPTER 11

ORION

I was at work a few weeks later, reviewing cost records with my father. The weather outside was unusually dark, and as I gazed out the windows that framed his huge corner office, my thoughts returned to my chat with Dr. Carlin. When I asked Dad, "What would you think about me going back to school?" he was staring at his computer, wrestling with a spreadsheet.

He appeared puzzled.

"For psychology," I clarified. "My therapist thinks I'd be good at it."

"That's a great idea," he said. "Really. I believe it's long overdue."

"What is?"

"Finding something you're passionate about." Dad leaned forwards. "What's David thinking?"

"Well, he loves the idea of me getting out of this job, that's for sure."

He tilted his head. "He doesn't really like me, does he?"

I shrugged. "He doesn't dislike you," I answered, skirting around the topic. "He just hates the music business."

"That's the problem with people like him," he replied, waving his hand dismissively. "Everything is black and white. "He doesn't understand that the world is mostly gray."

I shifted in my seat, eager to change the subject. "But that's why I love him so much," I corrected myself. "We balance each other."

Dad was silent.

"Anyway," I added, "I could probably use some structure, y'know? Going back to school would require a routine and a goal."

"Right up David's alley," Dad teased. "I'm sure he's thrilled."

"Actually, he's not," I said.

"Really?" he responded. "That surprises me."

It had startled me, too.

For months, I tried to put any ideas about education and sociopathy to one side. David started his new job shortly after, while I continued to work for my dad. I had to confess that things between us were no longer the same. David had been correct about the extended hours. He was rarely at home since he first started. He'd spend late hours and even entire weekends trapped in his new office while he and his team worked to deploy their Web application. It was a drastic change in our lifestyle, and I was unprepared. But I tried to make the most of it. At least I did at first.

During the first few months, I perfected the position of supporting partner. On nights when he worked late (which was the usual), I would make the lengthy drive to the other side of town so we could eat supper together, prepared foods in tow. I kept my mouth shut as hubby left for work on Saturday mornings. I tried not to get irritated when he called at the last minute to cancel dinner plans. I kept my complaints and thoughts to myself. But as time went, I found it more difficult to bite my lip.

"Are you fucking kidding me?" I mentioned this after David called one night to inform me—for the third time that week—that he would not be home for dinner. "You're doing this again?"

"I'm sorry, honey," he said. "I was literally walking out the door when Sam pulled me into a meeting."

Sam was David's employer and business partner. He was rigid and socially awkward, and lacked personality. Few individuals annoyed me more than Sam, and my dislike for him grew steadily.

I placed the bowl of whipped cream I was whisking on the kitchen counter, its sturdy base producing a loud thud. "Okay, I just finished making dessert. Homemade Key Lime Pie. I had to walk all the way downtown to find the proper limes." I sighed impatiently, my voice becoming somewhat softer. "Can't you just say we've got plans? Can't you simply say no? "Just this once?"

"I would if I could," he continued, clearly trying to get me off the phone. "But Sam is freaking out about the launch next week..." "Listen, it's just one more week," he said. "After that, things will return to normal. "I promise."

To his credit, things returned to normal the next week, and everything was perfect again. Around six p.m., he'd get home and we'd have supper, watch the news, and go about our usual routine. However, "normal" never seemed to last. The next week, he was back to working around the clock, this time for a "quarterly update" that had to be completed by the end of the month. That was what I despised most about his work. There was never a finish line. He'd kill himself to finish a major endeavor, only to quickly begin another. He kept insisting that Sam had promised that this would be the "last time," but it never was. I tried to be helpful, but after a while, I began to feel bitter.

This sucks, I told myself.

I returned home alone after another last-minute late-meeting phone call. The table was lit by candles, but the roasted halibut I'd made was cold and the veggies wilted. I took David's glass of wine and drank the contents. Then I entered the living room. I made my way to the window seat, rebelliously turning up the volume on the record player. I peered across the street and wished the Tarzana house was still unoccupied, or that its new owners hadn't been paranoid freaks who had installed a slew of surveillance cameras.

I laid my head against the wall while hypnotic blues and bass tones flooded the room. I looked into the kitchen and saw the pyramid of apples I'd carefully arranged on a vintage cake stand. And I started thinking of the movie Beaches. In the film, Barbara Hershey's character (Hillary) gives up a law career to establish a comfortable house for her prosperous husband. One morning, on his way out the door to work, the spouse inquires about her plans for the day.

"I'm going to buy a wrench," she informs him.

The spouse considers for a second before saying, "Super!"

Hillary gives a faint smile. In the scene's eating room, a platter of apples sits next to a pitcher of coffee. She takes one and places it on top of her head, looking straight ahead as her husband departs for work.

My eyes squinted as I looked at my own Apple Tower. I got up from the seat and proceeded to the kitchen. I picked a ripe Granny Smith and leaned over the island counter. I chewed into the apple and balanced it on top of my head.

"Maybe I should buy a wrench," I mumbled. It sounded like a good concept. One that would not have been entirely out of character. A significant part of me wanted to hurry out and get the wrench right then. I could see a variety of applications for it. Most notably against the side of Sam's car, which I knew was parked next to David's at the workplace.

However, something told me that Hershey's character was not going wrench shopping for some undetermined, enthrallingly antisocial duty. She was doing it because she had nothing else to do. And I was outraged because I could instantly connect. David's claim that he wanted us to live regular lives was true, but his definition of normal was not the same as mine. He worked around the clock to attain his objectives. So, why can't I do the same?

I attempted to talk to him about it, but he was constantly engaged with work. There was no "good time" to talk. When I tried to bring it up, he just became annoyed.

An hour later, I was behind the wheel of my automobile, my thoughts muddled as I drove home. It was late afternoon, the worst time to get caught in Los Angeles traffic. As I walked, I reflected on our chat and why the prospect of going to school scared him so much. Part of me got it.

It's kind of crazy, I thought. I am not even an excellent student.

Nonetheless, I had spent years researching sociopathy and psychology on my own. Going to graduate school seemed like a natural step. Difficult, but doable. Deep down, I knew I'd be good at it.

I took the 405 out of Brentwood and chose to bypass the freeway. Instead, I continued to Westwood, deep in meditation. When I arrived in Hilgard, I stopped at the red light and laid my head against the seat, lost in memories. I was probably more familiar with the intersection than everyone else in town. My first address in Los Angeles was on Hilgard Avenue. I gazed down the street toward where my dorm had been. A lot has changed since my arrival. The street seemed larger than I had remembered. The entire campus appeared to have burst in construction. But some things stayed the same.

I tightened my grip on the steering wheel and jerked it, turning off Sunset onto my old street. The granite wall that framed the campus's north side shone with large gold letters. UCLA. The large roadway was vacant and welcome, and I felt an unexpected sense of freedom. A hundred yards down was a side road that I remembered vividly. I pulled rapidly onto the narrow route and drove my car toward the nearby parking structure. I knew it was the one nearest to the psychology department.

Thirty minutes, I reasoned as I pulled into a parking space. The building will close in thirty minutes. There's plenty of time to see if Dr. Slack is available to meet with me.

When I got out of the automobile, the early evening air made me feel at ease. I looked up and automatically searched for Orion. I smiled to myself. This, I already knew, was the correct decision. I made a life-changing decision. I went to the psychology building with a plan in mind.

"I'm going to get my PhD," I resolved. "And I'm going to specialize in sociopathy."

Whether impulsive or not, the route of my future was evident. I was already gone.

CHAPTER 12

REBEL TELL

A year and a half later, I was standing in the living room of a rundown cottage off Mulholland Drive. There was a hole in the ceiling, and I could see the faint trace of a crescent moon against the bright California sky.

The residence wasn't far from the campus where I'd recently begun my second year of graduate studies at a private school in West Los Angeles. It was unusual for me to take a break in those days, let alone spend time in a stranger's home. A heavy course load, combined with the long hours I worked as a music manager, absorbed most of my days, leaving little time for "unorthodox" tasks. But that afternoon, I made an exception. And I had company.

A new companion stood beside me. Her name was Everly. Everly, the lead vocalist of a band that I had recently added to my management roster, was my favorite client. She was a prolific songwriter and superb singer whose style was reminiscent of Mazzy Star and Courtney Love. In addition, she had recently published a demo that had several major labels buzzing. The singer and I had spent a lot of time together preparing for her live performance, and for once, I was grateful for the company.

David was still working nonstop. His company was no longer a startup. It had grown into a thriving business that was preparing to go public. For more than a year, he'd been working virtually nonstop in preparation for the initial public offering, a move that was almost certain to secure his financial future and provide him true career freedom.

In terms of our careers, neither of us were simply existing. We were prospering. But it came at a high price. Between school and employment, David and I had become passing ships on a passive-aggressive ocean. We rarely spent time together, and when we did, we argued. Even after years of living with me, he couldn't believe that his "dream girl" was a sociopath. He didn't realize it had nothing to do with being a good or evil person. It was a personality type, and its characteristics were just part of my psychological makeup. I began to suspect that his acceptance of me had become conditional. He viewed my sociopathy as if it were a list of options, which he had no trouble cherry-picking.

David, I noted, was quick to express his displeasure with sociopathic actions he didn't appreciate. However, he was willing to adopt features of my personality type when it served his purpose. For example, he didn't seem to mind when I secretly punished individuals who I believed had harmed him. And he had no difficulty breaking into empty residences for sex. It was as if I couldn't be a psychopath without his consent, and the contradiction was frustrating. It was the same hypocrisy I had witnessed in society when it came to people like me.

Since discussing it with Dr. Carlin, I couldn't stop thinking about how my attributes were always viewed negatively. This viewpoint appeared shortsighted to me. Certainly, some of them could be utilized in a disastrous manner. However, as with any other trait, they can be employed constructively. For example, my decreased emotional capacity enabled me to make considerably more pragmatic decisions than, say, David, whose excess of emotion made him more prone to please others. Regarding my absence of remorse, I considered myself fortunate to have been spared such a burden.

The more time I spent studying psychology, the more convinced I became that shame was a state of mind created to enslave, not liberate. It seems to me that individuals didn't have to think for themselves as long as they felt guilty for doing so. And, while there was little research on sociopathy, there was plenty of information on the negative impacts of shame and guilt. From emotional reactions like low self-esteem and a proclivity for anxiety and melancholy to physical ones like increased sympathetic nervous system activity—including sleep and digestion problems—the negative features of guilt and shame appeared to outweigh the positive. My new friend agreed.

Everly was no stranger to the consequences of guilt. Despite being the main singer of a rising rock band, she frequently let others' opinions (and an excessive desire to be "good") sabotage her achievement. This stunned me. By all accounts, she was a wonderful person. Nonetheless, she was always fighting off thoughts of guilt. In many ways, she and David were similar. They were both extremely caring, compassionate, and loving. Both exhibited an abundance of compassion and emotional intelligence, which I thought to be my most lacking quality—the ability to connect and communicate through emotions. Both were extremely clever and talented. However, they were also constrained by what appeared to be an almost obsessive sense of morality. Everly was interested by the fact that I had never experienced anything like that before.

She once asked me, "Do you know how rare that is?" "Most individuals spend their entire lives attempting to rid themselves of guilt and shame. "I know I do," she said. "You're like a unicorn." Everly's acceptance of my sociopathic traits let me feel noticed in a positive light. Whereas David appeared focused on encouraging me to exhibit emotion and develop some sense of shame and remorse, Everly accepted me just as I was. As a result, I found it easier to accept myself.

"Being friends with you is like taking a guilt immunity pill," she added, glancing around the abandoned home. "Do you really believe I've ever broken into a house before? No way. I can't do things like this. But I can do it if you do." Then she said, "I love riding your dark coattails."

My phone started vibrating, and I checked to see whether David had sent me a text.

Good luck tonight, my darling. I can't wait to see you!

I smiled. David didn't like that I still worked for my father, so I was grateful that he was so supportive and came to the event.

I texted, "Thank you, Baby." I'm really excited!

"Is that David?" Everly asked. "He's coming tonight, right?"

"Of course," I replied, putting away my phone. "He just has to come straight from work."

She shakes her head. "Your boyfriend works more than anyone I've ever met," she told me. "Seriously, if Ben spent as much time at work as David, I'd be showing up at his office like Glenn Close in Fatal Attraction."

Ben was Everly's lover and one of her bandmates. He also served as her self-appointed "business manager." He was innocuous enough, but there were a few things about him that bothered me. For starters, I didn't appreciate how he made jokes at her expense, often in front of his "friends," a rotating cast of wannabe insiders. He fought any attempts I made to promote Everly as a solo artist, and he never seemed to pay attention to her unless it was related to the band.

I rolled my eyes at the idea of anyone giving a shit where Ben was, which Everly mistook for criticism.

"Don't judge me!" She laughed. "You know how jealous I am. "I wish I was more like you." She wrapped her arms over my neck. "My feisty little kitten!"

"Stop it," I said, trying to get away. Everly knew how much I disliked hugs.

"I can teach you a thing or two," she explained. "Things like love and affection!" She pressed an overdone kiss into my cheek. "Symmetrical symbiosis!" she exclaimed. "Put us together and we're the perfect person!"

I broke loose and laughed. "That's enough education for today." I glanced at my watch. "Anyway, we need to get going. "Sound check is in 30 minutes."

"Yes!" Everly exclaimed, her blue eyes blazing. "Let's go play a rock show."

Later that night, I sat backstage in the Roxy dressing room, reviewing the guest list. Despite my introverted disposition, I found my job as a rock band manager to be an odd fit for me. There was never any standing room for me during Everly's gigs, no chance for someone to approach me or start a long chat. Except for the few contacts with music industry professionals I had invited, I kept my eyes down and my hands occupied. I never stopped to get a drink while working on one of Everly's performances. Not until roughly 20 minutes before the show. That's when I'd go upstairs and collapse on one of the couches for a little pre-set cat nap.

The modest dressing room was packed that night. I set the list aside and laid my head on the arm of a couch, my eyelids heavy with the subtle hum of murmured talk.

"Hey," murmured Tony, prodding me with his toe. I opened my eyes and grinned at the band's road manager, who never failed to make me laugh with his sharp wit and adorable smile. "You gonna sleep through the show?"

"No way," Everly jokes, winking at me. "Patric just likes to hide."

"Rest in peace."

The door to the dressing room swung open. "I'm here!" said a short, obnoxious man. "Now the show can start." Dale was one of Ben's industry mates. However, I had yet to determine which industry. He was a walking, talking embodiment of every Los Angeles cliché. I couldn't deal with him.

"Sorry I'm late," he said, tugging conspicuously on his nose. "It took me an hour to find a parking space. I ended up parking my car halfway up Wetherly."

"Wetherly?" Ben yelped. "There's only residential parking up there. "You are going to get a ticket!"

"Patric," he grumbled, evidently frustrated that I hadn't guessed the outcome. "Can you please get Dale a parking pass?"

"Of course," I replied, moving from the couch. "Give me your keys, and I will handle it. "What kind of car?"

Dale gave me a smug look and tilted his head forward. He was sporting a baseball cap imprinted with a bright metallic Z. He pointed to it and raised his eyebrows, waiting for my response. I shook my head to signify that I did not identify the symbol. "I have no idea what that is."

"It's a Z," Dale said incredulously. "A Nissan Z?"

"Oh, just give Patric your keys," Everly explained. "We don't want you getting a ticket."

Dale smirked at her before reaching into his pocket and pulling out a set of keys. The ring featured a huge silver Z, which he hung in front of me like a dime store hypnotist. I tried not to laugh. Instead, I casually grabbed the keys. But just as I was about to go for the ring, he snapped it away from me.

"Not a chance, doll," he muttered, flinging them to a neighboring coffee table. "No one touches the Z." He paused. "But I will take a drink," he said.

Everly recoiled. "Dale," she murmured, breaking all pretense of civility. "Patric isn't a waitress."

Realizing he'd overplayed his hand, Dale placed his palms in front of his lips, his eyes wide with phony regret. "Oh my God! I'm so sorry!"

"It's fine," Ben exclaimed. He murmured, "That's what she's here for."

"I actually don't mind," I explained to Everly. This was correct. I would have done almost everything to flee the room.

I felt my phone vibrate in my pocket. "Besides, David's calling," I remarked, taking a glance at the screen. "He is probably outside. I'm going to go get him."

"And a Jack and Diet for Dale!" Ben yelled as I left.

I dashed down the rear steps and made a beeline for the front, my phone still vibrating in my pocket. "Hey," I replied as I responded, "I'm on my way." I could hear David's voice, but due to the crowd, I couldn't understand what he was saying. "I'm walking out the door right now."

I strolled outside and searched the sea of faces for him, but he was nowhere to be found. That's strange, I thought. I looked down at my phone and noticed I had a text message.

Stuck at work. I am very sorry, honey! I promise I'll make it up to you; be nice!!!!!!

I breathed sharply. The message was not new. I had undoubtedly received dozens of texts like it in the last two months. However, something about it seemed particularly aggravating that night. I clenched the phone, my fingertips turning white with rage as I pivoted on my heel and returned inside.

The breeze whistled in approval as I approached the sports car and opened the door. I reclined in the driver's seat, resting my head on the headrest. The automobile, like many before it, felt like a decompression chamber. Only now, instead of fighting the feeling of disinterest, I was eager to embrace it.

It was a strange feeling. Sitting there, I felt anything but safe. If anything, I was flirting with disaster as I prepared to go on an unlawful and perilous journey.

Poor judgment and failure to learn from experience, I reasoned. Cleckley places it eighth on his list. From where I was seated, everything appeared to be correct. But I didn't care.

Something about this joyride seemed unique. It felt like a new type of freedom—an expanding gyre from which I could get a higher, more informed perspective. This was a more matured sense of liberation: one that comes from understanding myself and following my own impulses rather than trying to please others. I may have been up to my old tactics, but this time I wasn't pacifying myself or attempting to keep from boiling over. I wasn't even doing it because I just wanted to break some regulations. I was doing it for one sole reason: to rebel.

Despite our wonderful honeymoon, my connection with David was becoming stifling. I deeply loved him, but it was just too much. The strain of feeling as if I had to comply with his standards and expectations made me angry. And not just any fury, but a certain kind of rage. It was a sharp spear of wrath fashioned in my upbringing, the scars of which I had spent the majority of my adult life attempting to forget.

I'd been trying to keep myself under control since David arrived in town. Restrained. To become the good young girl he desired. And that was okay. But this was much better.

"Be good," I mocked again, inserting the key into the ignition. "Where's the fun in that?"

I pushed the shifter into drive and pressed the accelerator. As I accelerated down the slope, the automobile let out a pleasant whine. I knew exactly what David would say if he discovered what I was up to.

You don't need to do this.

But that was the issue. Because, with the city streets at my mercy, I didn't feel the same way I had before. David was correct. I did not have to do it.

I could not wait to do it.

CHAPTER 13

SMOKE AND MIRRORS

It was safe to say things were not going well. My personal life was a mess. David and I seldom spoke. My extracurricular activities were really questionable. I was seriously considering committing myself to a mental facility.

It had been weeks since I had visited Dr. Carlin. Between my job, school, and my regular visits to Ginny's backyard, I hardly had time to eat, let alone go back and forth to the other side of town for treatment. This was unimportant, however, because as my sociopathic behavior manifested itself, my decision to distance myself from her was motivated by self-preservation rather than logistics. The fact that the majority of my leisure time was spent testing the Tarasoff rule meant that my therapist was no longer an acceptable confidant.

I was on my own.

My fingers rushed over the keyboard, and the buttons clicked sharply. It was the morning after my visit to Ginny's house, and instead of working, I was at my desk looking up "modern asylums." My actions the night before had left me unnerved. What had begun as a harmless stretch of sociopathic muscle had evolved into something I wasn't sure I could handle. I was concerned at how rapidly my objectives had moved from disciplined transgression to near ferocity. In the light of day, it became clear: I required substantial expert assistance. I was willing to do almost everything to get it.

"Anorexia," as I read, "bipolar, depression." My eyes scanned the list of illnesses addressed at a famous northern California wellness center. I frowned as I scrolled down the list. "Schizoaffective disorder, schizophrenia, social anxiety disorder, Tourette's syndrome."

"Fuck," I mumbled, unhappy at the lack of sociopathy among the alternatives. Just like dictionaries.

I scratched off another name from the spreadsheet I had printed. It was ranked thirty-third on my list. In the few hours since I began, my search for expert intervention had yielded no feasible options. None of the psychiatric treatments listed on the mental facility websites provided therapy for sociopathy. Nobody at the many businesses I called could even point me in the proper direction. Sociopathy was "clinically obsolete," according to one woman. She had unhelpfully claimed that schizophrenia was extremely common.

"Are you hearing voices?" the woman inquired. And I said "no" before I had time to think about it.

Cleckley ranked "absence of delusions and other signs of irrational thinking" second on his list. The psychologist hypothesized that sociopaths do not exhibit psychotic symptoms in the same manner as schizophrenics do. As a result, they have logical reasoning abilities and are thought to be in control of much of their antisocial behavior. In other words, sociopaths are tempted to commit violent acts because they believe they want to, not because they hear voices urging them to.

"Patric," my assistant said over the intercom, "your dad wants to see you."

I took a big breath and got up from my desk.

Maybe I should pretend to be crazy, I thought as I strolled down the corridor. After all, I heard voices. My own. They were inciting me to do bad things to Ginny Krusi.

Dad responded, "Hey," as I shuffled into his office. "I need you to check on the Hudson demo." The Hudson demo consisted of tracks from a pop group we represented. Dad had waited weeks for it to be finished. It was nearing the end of production in a Hollywood recording studio.

I didn't acknowledge him because I was still thinking about how to provide a convincing schizophrenia impression.

"Patric," Dad said. "Are you listening to me?"

"Yeah," I replied. "Sorry, I am just bewildered. Are you sure it's finished?"

"No," he yelled, "but I need it to be done. I'm meeting with three labels next week. So, if I have to send you to the studio every goddamn day to badger them about it, I'll do it."

It was a short trip to the studio. I waved at the receptionist in the foyer before walking down the long main corridor in search of the Hudson team. I'd been interested in recording studios since I was a child, and my father would take me with him to work. They reminded me of creative caves—always dark, cold, and filled with music. You never knew what you would find.

After a few minutes of searching, I came upon a producer I recognized. He was resting against an open studio door, facing me, while standing casually inside the frame, talking to someone I couldn't see.

He remarked, "Hey, Patric," as I approached. "What's up?"

"Hey, Neil," I said with a smile. "You haven't seen Bill around, have you?" I inquired, referring to the lead producer. "I'm trying to track down a demo."

Just then, another man appeared from inside the studio. An acoustic guitar draped from a heavy strap across his shoulder, and I recognized him right away, despite the fact that he was taller than I expected.

"Hi," he said.

"Oh, I'm sorry," Neil said. "Do you guys know each other?"

The guy shakes his head. He moved confidently into the corridor and extended his hand. I laughed. I'd never become accustomed to being presented to someone whose identity was evident. Despite growing up in the entertainment industry and spending most of my adult life working in close proximity to a wide range of successful musicians, the ritual of the introduction—as if the name of the person standing in front of me wasn't comically obvious—has always struck me as amusing. I resolved to say just that to the man with the guitar.

"I never thought about that," he added, smiling. "So, how about this," he suggested, his eyes twinkling mischievously. "Pretend I'm not me." He extended his other hand and announced, "My name is Max. Maximum Magus."

"Nice," I replied, playing along. "Like a Batman villain with a hint of porn."

"Your turn," he said.

"I'm Patric," I said.

He nodded his approval. "So, tell me, Patric, do you know any good places to eat around here?"

I nodded. "Yes."

"Well, what do you say about lunch?"

I shook my head, amazed but somewhat scared off by his assurance. "Thanks for the invitation," I added with a grin, "but my boyfriend frowns on me going on lunch dates with strange men."

"Oh, great boyfriend placement," he responded without skipping a beat. "You see what she did there, Neil?" he inquired. "She let me know she was taken, and so smoothly. But the joke is on you, he replied, "because I, too, have a significant other."

"How nice for her!" I exclaimed, chuckling.

"So, how about it?" he inquired. "Now that you understand I'm not hitting on you, it's completely innocent. Besides, I'm starving, and Neil refuses to accompany me."

"I'm in the middle of mixing your album," Neil lamented. Max waved his hand dismissively.

"I can't," I said. "I work, too. I am merely here to find a demo."

"Mike!" Max let out a startled shout.

Another man appeared at the doorway. "What's up, boss?"

"I need you to track down a demo." Max glanced at me hopefully.

I sighed, pretending frustration. "It's the band Hudson," I explained, apologizing to Mike. "Bill Gross is the producer."

Mike picked up the phone. "Give it one second. "I'll call the engineer."

"Looks like you're out of excuses."

"I really have to get back to work," I told myself.

"Me, too," he insisted.

"But if you feel like waiting around for me to drop off the demo," said I, "there's a place near my office called the Smoke House."

Later that night, I sat in the living room, waiting for David to arrive home. I'd poured two glasses of wine and, as I rested on the window bench facing the street, I couldn't help but feel content from my lunch with Max. I'd begun the day depressed, resigned to the prospect of submitting myself to a mental institution. But suddenly, I felt absolutely clear. I hadn't been seeking one, but Max had proven to be an excellent acceptance surrogate. Hanging out with him had been enjoyable. Unexpectedly. For the first time in months, I had the opportunity to simply be myself, as I liked myself. And I hoped to keep the enthusiasm going with David.

The weather was cool, and I had opened the French doors to the backyard. A flaming log in the fireplace crackled, jazz played from the speakers, and I felt like I was going to explode with relief. Twenty-four hours ago, I stood beneath a canopy of tree branches, inches from committing a big mistake. But now I can't see doing anything like that. The desire to go to Ginny's house—to do anything terrible, in fact—was as far from me as a Louisiana Baptist hymn, a dim memory from my adolescence.

I laid my head against the picture window. A gentle glow illuminated the canyon road underneath. When I saw David's headlights, I raced out of my seat. I closed the shutters, ran to turn off the stereo, and grabbed the other glass of wine as I dashed to the door. I'd arranged to meet him in the driveway. I had planned to greet him with a glass of wine as soon as he stepped out of his car. But in my haste, I neglected to put down my own glass. With both hands full, I had no way of opening the door. I bent at the waist and attempted to twist the doorknob with my shoulder. However, I couldn't pull it open before David's shadow emerged in the frosted window of the door panel.

"Patric?" he inquired through the door. "What the hell are you doing?"

I laughed and straightened up as he pushed open the door. "I was gonna meet you outside," I began, "except I didn't have any hands."

He laughed and shut the door. "Well, this is nice," he exclaimed, gladly receiving the drink. "Why are you still awake?" "It's nearly midnight."

I threw my arm around his neck and drew him into a lengthy kiss. "I know," I replied. "I figured you might be hungry."

"Mmmm... I am starving," he stated.

"There's chicken pot pie in the oven."

He smiled. "That's not what I meant."

Hours later, we were lying in bed. He carefully listened as I recounted the events of my afternoon. He nodded as I told him about my trip to the studio and my chance encounter with the curious musician.

"So... like, the two of you are friends now?" he was asking.

"I wouldn't go that far," I replied, chuckling. "But he invited us to a show at the Bowl." I shake my head. "Isn't that awesome?"

"Well, I don't love you getting randomly drunk with the guy in the middle of the afternoon."

"Oh, live a little." I nudged him. "Besides, it wasn't like that."

"Uh-huh," he replied. "So, what was it like?"

I attempted to figure out how to explain it. "Today, hanging out with this stranger, I could simply be myself. It wasn't important who he was. I didn't care if he was a talking robot or not. It was just good to be able to discuss my diagnosis with someone and use the term sociopath without feeling horrible."

"You told him that?" David inquired, surprised. "Why?"

"Because this is who I am, honey. "This is my life," I informed him. "And it was fun! That is why I was in such a fantastic mood throughout the day. It felt liberating. It's liberating to feel welcomed."

"I accept you," David responded calmly.

"Not always," I responded in kind.

He cocked an eyebrow. "What an exciting life he must have," he remarked, shifting the topic.

I glanced at him with terror. "Are you kidding?" All he does is compose, record, and tour. Write, record, and tour. Where's the normalcy? "Where is life?" I shake my head. "Do you think any of those people—artists, specifically—get to have normal relationships or lives? Consider how ephemeral their existence must be. It's as if the moment someone decides to be an artist, whether successful or not, they cease progressing alongside the rest of society. They are caught in a situation of suspended impermanence."

David smiled. "I guess I never considered it that way. But I really like how you thoroughly evaluate everyone you meet."

"Because it fascinates me! That's what I enjoy about school. I had no idea about any of this before, including the people. I'd only ever researched sociopathy before. But now I'm learning about the many personality kinds. All the various methods in which people deal with their psychological limitations. "I feel like I can't get enough." I locked eyes with him. "People are fucking amazing, you know?"

He smiled faintly and placed a lock of hair across my forehead. "I'm proud of you," he stated. "The work you do on yourself, getting a PhD… It's amazing." He paused. "I think you are amazing."

I grinned and fought back against the slight tug of duty. I was well aware that I hadn't actually kept my part of the arrangement. I hadn't informed him about Ginny, my visits to her condo, or how I had spent the morning seeking a mental facility. But I also realized it wasn't safe. Not yet, anyhow. And certainly not in that moment, when everything was so calm and perfect.

"So what about tomorrow?" I asked enthusiastically. "Could you come home first, and we can go together? "Or do you want to meet me at the Bowl?"

He gave a sad expression. "Oh, honey," he replied. "I can't go tomorrow night. "Do you remember the company dinner?"

"Dammit," I mumbled. "I forgot." I leaned against him and sighed. "Nevermind, then," I replied. "I'll just meet you at the restaurant."

I could feel him shake his head. "Honey, no," he said. "It's a fucking work party with the most uninteresting people on Earth. "Escape while you can."

I collapsed into his chest, my body succumbing to tiredness. "Well, when you put it that way," I said.

"Just be good," he whispered, sleepily.

CHAPTER 14

TRANSPARENCY

Later that night, I sat across from David at the dining room table. By all accounts, it had been a wonderful evening. I'd arrived home in time to prepare supper, and David—who'd recently completed a large project—was in a good mood. At least he was at the beginning.

"I've decided to include my sociopathic diagnosis in my dissertation defense," I stated over dessert.

He paused mid-chew and had the arrogance to appear perplexed. "Huh?"

"Going forward I want to be more transparent about the fact that I'm a sociopath," I told you. "It makes no sense to conceal it." Especially if I ever want to be a voice for those like me." I paused to let my enthusiasm settle in. "I think it could be the start of something really cool."

He shook his head and gulped hard. "So now you want to tell everyone?"

I exhaled. It was a rerun of an argument we'd had for years. He was bothered by my urge to "lean in" to my personality type. Not only did he oppose my decision to reveal my condition in my dissertation, but he now refuses to discuss it. The conversation lasted only a few minutes before he became enraged and went off to the bedroom.

I looked at the taper candles that shone in the center of the table. Bright orange flickers created relaxing dark shadows on the wall. Everly was correct, I thought. I adored David, but I was done coasting with him. I wanted our relationship to succeed, to be a true collaboration. It was time to be myself. And it felt nice to be free.

I regarded the candles for a few more seconds before regretfully extinguishing them. I cleared the table and began tidying up. I took my time filling the dishwasher. I carefully wiped down the island and counters. Only then did I turn out the lights and head to my bedroom.

The door was closed. I slowly opened it and discovered that David was already in bed. "Honey," I stated quietly, "I adore you. But what happened just now is exactly why I want to be more honest about who I am."

He turned his head to stare up at the ceiling. "What do you mean?" he inquired with a sad sigh.

"You refuse to discuss the fact that I am a sociopath." I can't even bring it up without making you upset. "And I understand," I said. "You don't want me to be a sociopath since they're known for being awful. And you don't want to see that side of me."

He pressed himself up against the pillows. "I don't see those parts of you," he insisted. "I mean, I've seen you do awful things, but I don't consider you bad, Patric. Tell me you know that."

"I know that," I said. "I can't express how much I appreciate hearing those things. I'm not sure how much your opinion of me as something other than a 'bad girl' influenced my self-awareness. You have transformed my life." I smiled weakly. "But not everyone has someone like you in their lives, honey. Not everybody has a David. And I want to help others who are not as fortunate as myself."

He thought about it. "I hear you," he finally said. "And I get it. Of course, I think striving to help others is admirable. I really do. But how would it work if you tell everyone you're a sociopath?" he inquired. "Once you say that, no one will listen to anything else you say. Each data point will be examined. Every tale you tell will be questioned. Sociopaths have long been seen as untrustworthy sources, let alone doctors. He paused. "They're just gonna hate you."

122

"Who cares?" I responded. "At the end of the day, all I can do is speak the truth. I have no influence over how people choose to accept the facts. Other sociopaths won't dislike me. They are going to see themselves. Finally."

He remained quiet for a few seconds. "I don't know about this, honey," he eventually said. I shake my head.

"That's the thing," I informed him. "You don't need to know. It doesn't matter if you agree with me. David, it's my decision. I folded my hands in my lap. "And I've made it."

Even as I spoke, I could feel compassion seeping from his face. "So how I feel doesn't matter," he remarked, shaking his head.

I grimaced with disappointment. We had come so close.

He pursed his lips. "Why are we even together?" he questioned rhetorically.

"You tell me," I said softly.

David's eyes widened, and he almost shouted, "I don't know! It's not like we see each other any longer. I'm working my ass off, and it feels like it's for nothing. We can't even eat supper without bickering over the same crap." He breathed forcefully. "Why don't we have normal difficulties, you know? "Like a normal fucking couple."

"Normal?" Now I was outraged and trying not to yell. "Where did you get the idea? Was this when we met? When was I grabbing maps and hiding in a basement? Or all those times on the phone when I told you I suspected I was a sociopath?" I extended out my hands, feigning interest. "Maybe it was the GODDAMN KEYCHAIN I FOUND IN THE HOUSE ACROSS THE STREET TO LET YOU KNOW WHEN I'M DOING FUCKED-UP SHIT!" I pointed my finger at David. "No," I replied sharply. "When you arrived, you recognized me right away. You knew I was FAR FUCKING FROM

NORMAL. It's simply that once you had me, you realized you didn't want me!"

"That's not true!" he insisted. "I only want the real you. I want you to be the person I know you are on the inside. He shook his head, sadly. "I know she is in there. "I know it, Patric."

I stared at the floor. "Oh my God," I exclaimed. "David. I am not doing this with you anymore." I put one hand on my chest. "For the final time." There is only one me. This describes who I am. And I can't continue to repress it because you don't like it." I shook my head, helplessly. "I cannot change my personality, David. However, you have the ability to choose how you will react to me. And if you don't understand—or can't or won't—I'm not sure what to say. I am done. "I don't care anymore."

"You've made that pretty fucking clear," he muttered.

I wasn't sure what to say. I cared about David. I cared about him more than I ever had before. But if he doesn't know that... If he still didn't get it...

"Maybe you're right," he continued, his voice softer. "Maybe we shouldn't do this anymore."

I stared him in the eye. He felt quite sad and angry. I gently shook my head, puzzled. "I never said that."

He scowled. "You may as well have."

"But I didn't," I answered calmly. "So, if that's how you feel—if you believe we shouldn't be together—then you should express it. You should embrace your sentiments rather than transferring them onto me."

"Fine," he said. "That's how I feel." I feel as if I don't matter. I get the impression that you don't care. Then he stared at me, enraged. "Am I wrong?"

It was one last opportunity for me to intercede and resolve things, as I always did. One final passive-aggressive demand for me to make him feel better, to assure him that everything would be fine, that I would change, and that we could work it out. But I didn't feel tempted to give in. So I just sat down. It felt great to be impermeable.

David, seemingly unhappy that I did not answer, blinked away his tears and fumed in silence. He leaned over and turned off his bedside lamp, plunging the room into darkness. With an audible exhale, he aggressively rolled to his side. Then he pulled the comforter across his shoulder. All the while, I stared blankly at the wall in front of me.

After a few seconds, I stood up. I changed my clothing, brushed my teeth, and went to bed. I looked up at the ceiling, the house's oppressive silence wrapping around me. I felt like I should've been sad, but I wasn't. In reality, I was relaxed.

It felt lovely to feel nothing.

CHAPTER 15

KILLER QUEEN

David moved out that weekend. I despised watching him pack. I realized I should have been upset. And I was upset. I just couldn't relate to the feeling. It was like chewing something I couldn't taste, which just exacerbated my displeasure.

"Are you certain this is what you want?"" he inquired, after packing the rest of his belongings into his car.

"No."

He appeared crushed. It reminded me of our first breakup, when we were teenagers.

"I love you, Patric," he stated. He placed his hands on my hips and crushed his forehead against mine, and for a moment I thought I would cry. But I did not. The sensation arose and faded before I could feel it, like it had done countless times before. David eventually got in his car and drove away.

Standing there, watching him go, I realized the time had arrived. Watching David depart should have been enough to make me feel anything. I believed it was now or never. I planted my feet, ready to burst into sobs. I stood in the driveway for around twenty minutes before giving up. There was no emotion waiting in the wings for the proper opportunity to emerge. I felt as I always did. Ambivalent. I turned around and went back home.

I shut the door behind me and embraced the silence of my now-empty home. It felt thick, like a weighted blanket, and I was sleepy. I sat on the couch, gazing at the floor till my eyes relaxed. I remembered the hidden-image posters, or stereograms, that used to be available in the mall. God, those posters irked me. No matter how hard I tried, I couldn't shift my focus to expose the tiger or the rose. I kept seeing the same thing: a meaningless mosaic of shapes.

The opposite was happening now. As I gazed at the patternless wooden boards, I felt disconnected from my thoughts. I let them float while my internal and exterior climates aligned. Instead of being frustrated by my inability to see something hidden, I allowed myself to accept that there was nothing there to see at all.

Who are you, Patric? My unconnected mind wandered. I was still not sure. But I was certain I was done looking to others for answers. Whether it was the desire for like-minded friends, relationships with nice people I could use as tethers to a "normal" existence, or surrogates I could utilize for my own self-acceptance, I'd always mistakenly imagined my "sociopath to enlightenment" trip would not be one I took alone. But now that I was alone, I saw what should have been evident all along.

"I don't care."

I didn't mind that there wasn't anyone else like me in my life. I didn't mind that I was alone.

Everyone else spent their lives trying to avoid sociopaths, but I'd always wanted to find them. While the other kids at school were playing sports, I was breaking into houses. While other girls were playing home and fantasizing about the day they would hear those "three little words," I had taken a different road. I, too, wanted to embrace "three little words." But mine were a little different.

"I do not care!"

A month later, I was in the administration office at school, going over PhD requirements with my supervisor. I'd noticed a "clinical" requirement in the graduation paperwork a few days before and called the office to inquire. Dr. Robert Hernandez, the chair of my department, had emphasized that, in addition to my coursework and dissertation, I needed to complete 500 hours as an intern to receive my PhD. In other words, I needed to "train" as a therapist for 500 unpaid hours. I wasn't pleased with it.

"Come on, Patric," he urged. Dr. Hernandez was an affable practitioner with a dry sense of humor. He taught my psychoanalysis class, and we had always gotten along. "Think of it as an exciting learning experience."

"Except, I don't want to learn," I muttered, crossing my arms. "I'd sooner open a vein than hear a bunch of Beverly Hills-adjacents complain about their first-world troubles. Not a joke. "I'll bleed out right here."

The doctor tried not to laugh. "Then please walk into the hallway first," he continued, "since we can't do anything about it. It is essential. You can complete the hours at any certified practice you like. But if I were you, I would just walk down the street."

I looked at him blankly.

"The counseling center," he said, as if I didn't understand.

"I know what 'down the street' is," I said, before changing tactics. "I apologize." Have you forgotten? "I'm a diagnosed sociopath," I said. "You guys shouldn't be letting people like me work as therapists... not for normal people anyway."

"Why not?"He asked. "You've said it a dozen times: you want to help others, right?"

"I want to help sociopaths," I explained. "Ideally, from a distance."

"Look at the bright side. "Half the battle in clinical training is helping trainees compartmentalize their own emotional attachments," he said, clearly enjoying himself. But you don't have any!"

"I'm glad you find this entertaining," I said, taking my luggage from beneath my chair. "For the record, I accept no responsibility here. Whatever happens, it is your responsibility." I turned and walked towards the door.

The Aloe Center provided psychiatric treatments to persons who did not have insurance or could not afford to pay out of pocket for one-on-one therapy, which was sometimes expensive. In many situations, the sessions were free. As a result, the patient population was highly diverse, both demographically and psychologically. We had everyone from underprivileged warriors dealing with PTSD to affluent victims of domestic violence who didn't want to be seen going to treatment anywhere near their Beverly Hills homes. Interns like me were plunged into the deep end of the pool in what amounted to a crash course on treating every conceivable problem.

Just a few weeks into my residency, I noticed a pattern. As the newest intern, I had the lowest rank on the case-assignment totem pole, which meant I frequently got patients that no one else wanted. This included patients with "excessive comorbidities"—a group of symptoms that overlapped and made diagnosis difficult. These were the patients who did not fall cleanly into any diagnostic category. The formula at the counseling facility was simple: assess, diagnose, treat, and repeat. Patients with symptoms that did not lend themselves to a clear and definite diagnosis flowed down to me. Right away, I noticed personality features that I recognized. Although they were first hesitant to speak frankly, several of them finally admitted to feelings of "emotional emptiness" and a desire to do "bad things." They described deviant behavior and a clear inability to connect with remorse. These patients described violent behavior and trouble controlling their impulses. They admitted to deception for the sake of fitting in. They told story after story about attempting to overcome their emotional paralysis through pain and harmful behavior. They discussed dark secrets and compulsive behavior. Even though some admitted to many crimes, none had a criminal record. Some were married with children. Most of them had college degrees. Everyone was living a lie.

These individuals had many of the same characteristics from Cleckley's checklist as I did. They grappled with remorse. They felt detached from their feelings. They discovered serenity amidst pandemonium. They derived satisfaction from confrontation. In spite of their darkness, these individuals expressed strong feelings of love and affection. They understood the concept of empathy and could convey compassion. They could express frankly to me their wish to understand themselves and break the pattern of their harmful conduct. They displayed politeness and cooperation. They were friendly. They donated to charities. They were conscientious. They were self-aware. And they were afraid.

The majority of these patients were familiar with the term "sociopath." They, too, had recognized themselves in pop-culture renderings of the term and were alarmed by what they discovered. They feared they were monsters. They were frightened that time was running out. Many of them had already seen multiple therapists, only to leave feeling useless and alone, just like I had. They, too, struggled with destructive compulsions that were becoming increasingly difficult to manage. These people needed someone who could understand and listen without judgment. What they needed was assistance. All they needed was hope. They needed an advocate. They got me.

An hour later, I hung up and relaxed back in my chair. Parking cops, sleep well tonight, I reasoned comfortably. The late afternoon sun threw deep shadows over my office, and I sighed contentedly. Teri had been my last appointment of the day, and I was eager to be done.

I wonder what would happen if I stayed here for one night. I thought. The idea was quite appealing. It's not exactly a suite at the Ambassador, I remarked with a smile. But it might be intriguing.

My phone buzzed, and I noticed a text from Max.

Knock, knock.

He'd been back in LA for a few weeks, although it didn't seem like we'd spent much time apart. In fact, we'd been texting virtually nonstop since his departure. It was a mode of communication that I saw as both liberated and constraining. I'd spend hours messaging him about everything from my attempts at psychotherapy to his different romantic interests. It provided for the one-sided engagement that I preferred. I appreciated being with someone who did not want to change me, marry me, or think about "the future" or anything more sophisticated than the next chord progression.

But since he returned to town, the dynamic has changed. We had begun hanging out more frequently, and I wasn't sure how I felt about it. Prior to my separation with David, I understood exactly where Max fit in my life and how to administer my medication. I had a boyfriend, but it wasn't Max. But now everything was different. Our relationship was hard to describe. The lines had blurred. Perhaps they had always been blurred. Again, I was unable to tell.

Max poked his head inside my office door when it cracked open. "Knock, knock," he repeated.

"Jesus!"I exclaimed. The therapists' offices were only accessible via several locked doors. "How did you get back here?""

"The chick in front buzzed me through." He sat down on the couch in front of me.

"I'm sure she did," I remarked dryly.

"So, what's happening?He asked. "Where do we go?"

We had planned to meet for drinks after work. But I did not feel like drinking. I wrinkled my nose at him. "I don't know," I replied. "I'm not in a bar-ish mood."

"My house, then," he said, too abruptly. "It's perfect, actually. Max's "music room" was a windowless cave with an incredible collection of musical instruments and memorabilia. I have a tune I'd like to play for you there. It was hard to enter the music room without immediately losing track of time, which he frequently used to his advantage.

"Hostage theater," I added, smirking. It was how I described the frequently oppressive experience of being compelled to listen to new music. It has always been my least favorite aspect of being a manager.

"Fuck off!"" he responded, laughing.

"I swear to God, all you artists are the same," I quipped. "It doesn't matter if you've sold one song or ten million. When a musician wants to perform you a song, it's like being held at gunpoint.

"Fortunately for me," I added, "I don't have to do that anymore. I am no longer a manager, remember?"

Max, unlike David, passionately opposed my choice to quit. He gave a sneer. "Not true," he corrected me. "Isn't your friend's last gig tomorrow night?"

I nodded, grudgingly. Everly's final Roxy appearance would signal the official end of her time with the band. It was bittersweet because, while I was ready to leave the music profession for good, I was unsure how Everly would react.

"Yeah," I responded.

"So technically, you are still a music manager. Not that it matters. I'm not interested in your professional opinion." He smiled triumphantly and got from the couch. "So come on," he said. "You can follow me."

I gazed out the window of my office and noticed the mountains that framed the northside of Beverly Hills. I had an idea.

"Actually," I explained, "you can follow me."

I knew what being with Max would be like. It would be enjoyable. Fun, inventive, wild, extreme, unrestrained, and inculpable. I wouldn't have to work a single day in my life if I spent it with Max— literally or metaphorically. I could disappear into the existence that my dark side desired. She was tugging at me now, literally salivating at the egocentric jugular Max had revealed. "Do it," she pushed. Bleed him. Use him. I considered how simple it would be to utilize Max's three small words to hide my own.

There was no hesitation in his voice when he uttered it. Only confidence. He moved to face me, his lips caressing my temple. I raised my chin to gaze at him. Staring into his eyes brought back memories of the Great Blue Hole. And as he kissed me, I wanted to sink.

Max's flavor—an agonizing combination of salt, licorice, and whiskey—was everything my shadow self had convinced me I'd always desired. An inviting abyss. Freedom, pardons, and prizes oh my! For a brief while, I felt unstable due to the undeniable electricity we experienced.

Max raised his hands to either side of my face. I squeezed my eyes tightly shut. God, I thought. Why isn't this enough?

Life with someone like him was the road of least resistance. Max delighted in darkness rather than virtue. And there, in that darkness, I realized I could hide from reality. The reality was, I did love Max, but not in a healthy way. That was certainly not good. With him, I could stay exactly how I was. I would never be judged for being awful or urged to improve. But I did not desire a relationship like that. What I desired was a true collaboration. Beautiful, cooperative, tough, and additive. It's exactly what I wanted with David. That's all I've ever wanted. If I couldn't have what I wanted with the man I want...

I placed a hand on his chest and gradually pushed myself away. "No," I replied.

He was confused at first. He looked to the side and tightened his jaw, remaining silent for a few seconds. "Why?"He demanded.

"Because I don't want this."

"Bullshit," he exclaimed. "If you hadn't wanted it, we wouldn't be here!" He was upset. For a brief moment, I imagined my disinterest spreading throughout the house, devouring and negating his wrath.

"What were your thoughts?" I snapped, imitating his demeanor. "You were going to write me a song, tell me you love me, and we'd live happily ever after?"

"Perhaps I did!" he yelled. "What's wrong with that?""

"What's wrong is that I do not love you like that. I don't love anyone in that way, remember?"

"Yeah, I remember," he replied. "It's my favorite thing about you."

There it was. Max, I knew, didn't love me. He was in love with the fact that he believed I was incapable of loving. Not typically. Max understood that I would never judge him, be envious, or clingy. I would not mind if he was gone for months at a time. That kept me safe. To him, I represented a promise he did not have to keep. And to me, he was a safe haven from which I did not have to emerge. A dark and muddy cave where time stopped and consequences did not matter. As long as I had Max, I could remain in the shadows. I could keep looking for new medicines and standing stationary while pretending to move.

"Come on," I begged. "Don't blame me for telling the truth. You know as well as I do. This"—I extended my arm roughly about the area between us—"only works because we are friends."

"Friends?"Max responded with a snort. "That's cute."

"Don't be a dick," I replied. "We've always been friends."

Max went to the piano and slammed its lid shut. He turned to face me and added, "Trips to abandoned houses," with a sarcastic tone. "Late-night trips to strangers' backyards; sociopathic confessionals. He scoffed, "Is that what you do with your friends?""

I nodded. It was, actually.

He stabbed a finger at me and spat, "Then it's no wonder you don't have any."

He scowled at me for a moment. Then he turned on his heel and left. He threw open the door and marched to his car, almost tripping over something in the grass. The old man used to sit in a wooden chair outside, keeping his wife company. The coffee cup beside it was sun-bleached and shattered.

I waited until he drove away before carefully closing the door. After a few seconds, I climbed the stairs and entered the main bedroom. A four-poster bed was shoved against the far wall, and I sank into it. Above the headboard, there was a window that overlooked the street. I looked through the muslin curtains for a while, secretly watching passers-by. Then I fell asleep.

CHAPTER 16

RORSCHACH

I awoke to my phone buzzing against the floors. I blinked numerous times, trying to focus on the unfamiliar walls that surrounded me. For a little minute, I relished in not knowing where I was. Then I recalled everything. My phone vibrated again. I moaned and rolled across the mattress. Decades-old springs creaked in protest as I bent over the edge. I clicked "Answer" without looking at the screen and held the phone to my ear. "What time is it?""I asked.

"It's showtime!"Everly sang." "Can you believe it?" My final Roxy show. I'm stressed out. What time do you anticipate you'll arrive? I know we typically meet in the afternoon, but today you should arrive earlier." She hesitated. "Like, now."

I placed my palm over my eyes and despised the morning sun, which had already entered the small white chamber.

"I can't," I responded, unhappy with myself for sleeping late. "I have a shift at the counseling center and then I'm driving to the show with Dad." Everly was complaining. "Don't worry," I told her. "I'll have plenty of time to get to the Roxy before things get nuts."

"Fine, but you're coming to Dorian's after," she informed me. "No excuses."

I agreed and hung up, then rolled onto my stomach to gaze out the window. A woman was walking her dog down Benedict Canyon, and I liked knowing she couldn't see me. Alone in a stranger's bed, my existence unknown to the outer world, I felt more at ease than I had in a long time. I like being hidden, and—with Max's leaving words echoing in my ears—I began to believe it was definitely for the best. "It is no wonder I don't have any friends," I told him.

He was correct. My preferred activities, my reluctance to contribute, and my allergy to affection—none of these were conducive to a relationship. Not in the usual sense, anyway. I adored people. I really did. But the manner I loved was different from others. And, to be honest, we're not particularly compatible. I didn't need to receive love in order to give it. I never had. I preferred that my affections remain anonymous. Independent. Not because I didn't care, but because my concerns were different. I knew it better than anyone: the most appealing version of myself was the one seen from a distance.

I lay there for a while longer, soaking up the silence, comfortably cocooned in my apathy. Then I got up and went to the closet. "No sense going all the way back home," I murmured to the vacant house as I opened the door. A shoe rack hung inside, clattering as it swung. The outfits were largely men's. Pushing hanger after hanger aside, I'd almost surrendered myself to work pants and an old button-down. But then I saw the dress. It was a simple A-line with a dropped waist and lace neck. I smiled regretfully as I stroked my fingertip across the neckline, picturing the elderly woman who used to reside there. I think she looked nice in this.

I focused my attention on the shoe rack. Looking at a lovely pair of leather pumps, I scowled in dismay. My feet, I realized, were far too large. So I went with a somewhat bigger pair of men's oxfords and hefty socks. I took my time getting ready. When I finished, I looked in the mirror. Standing there in the ancient dress, with its floral print and classic form, I resembled a 1950s housewife rather than a twenty-first-century sociopath.

Invisible. My favorite thing to be. However, being invisible had its drawbacks. It's one thing to wear my own disguise, I reasoned, adjusting the pleats of the garment, and quite another to be assigned a costume.

I'd seen it happen with people who were aware of my diagnosis.

People were uncomfortable with portions of my personality that they couldn't or didn't want to see, so they would "dress me up," usually with their own preconceptions of how a sociopath should feel, behave, or react. The end outcome was a form of deception via proxy. People invented their own version of me and then blamed me when it failed. It was unpleasant and disruptive.

I carefully moved down the steps. Light cascaded from the hole in the ceiling into the living area, creating a waterfall effect. My gaze rested on the piano, and my thoughts clouded. The truth was that I was better off being alone. Not because I loathed people or friendship, but because I couldn't stop myself from being the person they thought I was. Unable to communicate through traditional ways, I realized long ago that my personality type may act as a mirror. I also understood that by leveraging it, I would be able to provide them with what they had long desired. Where better to hide than in plain sight? People were so captivated by my portrayal of their hobbies that they didn't notice when I sang off tune. Or they laughed too loudly. Or they cried too little. Or stared without blinking.

I considered it a superficial appeal. Cleckley ranked it first on his list as the fundamental attribute of the "classic" sociopath, indicating a glib, false interpersonal approach. That was accurate. Nobody seemed to understand, however, that this was not the result of a voluntary agreement with the devil. It was a coping strategy developed out of necessity. I seldom used charm as a trick. Like others in my cohort, I assumed I used it to hide, to mask my sociopathy, driven by a desire to survive. Not because I was terrified, but because I knew other people were. People eradicate what they fear. I considered cultivating.

My phone buzzed again, and I braced myself for another message from Max. But when I looked at the screen, I noticed a note from my father.

We'll pick you up at 9.

The sight of his text relaxed me. My dad would know what to do. His unwavering patience and judgment-free demeanor had always been a blessing. He had a rare ability to communicate with me while remaining impartial. He couldn't really relate, but he could reason. And that was exactly what I needed: someone who could argue without emotion. Free of feeling. Without an agenda.

"Welcome to the Roxy," a valet announced.

It took me a second to realize what was occurring. I shaded my eyes from the flickering lighting on the marquee. I had no notion that we had arrived. I felt disoriented. Disoriented and numb, I was desperate to get away from my father, who was unaware of the absurdity of his request.

The valet extended his hand, and I exited the car. Without turning back, I made my way to the box office, going through a long line that went around the block. I gave the doorman a short hello as he unhooked the velvet rope to let me in. Once inside, I was surrounded by people. I blinked in the dim light as I walked past the foyer. I felt invisible, but not in the manner I wanted. I felt blurry. The earth beneath my feet was shaky. As I approached the pub, I surveyed the throng for a familiar face—or one who would just acknowledge my presence. But I was alone.

For a moment, I pondered yelling. Or slamming the female in front of me so forcefully that her head snaps back. Or ripping the hairpin from her topknot and inserting it into the neck of the man standing next to her. Anything to get it to stop. The increasing stress. Criminal numbness. Emotional impoverishment.

Then I saw him.

"David!"I yelled.

He was standing at a bar table, his elbow delicately placed next to what I recognized as his famous gin and tonic. "David!" I cried again, almost yelling as I waved at him above the crowd. A mass of bodies threw me off balance, and I was swept sideways. But not until we locked eyes. He went forward and took my hand. Allowing him to rescue me from the sway, I took a moment to gather myself. I then wrapped my arms around him.

I said nothing as I stood there clinging on for dear life. I simply allowed myself to be held, snatched from the river, and briefly revived by David's presence.

"Hey," he said after a few seconds. "Are you alright?""

I muttered, "No," into his neck. "No. No. No. No." But the crowd's clamor drowned out my words.

David drew back to look at me. "Are you okay?""He asked again.

Looking up at him, the neon lights from the bar casting shadows across his face, it took all of my effort not to confess. Fall into his arms and ask him to save me. Tell him the truth. I loved him. I needed him. I ached for him. Not just because he was the one person who ever actually made me feel secure. And not just because being in his arms made me feel at home. But he was home. David was the best person I had ever known. The best person I've ever known. And who was I?

"I don't know," I responded gently. This was the problem. The reality was that there was no reality, unless I wanted to create one. The truth was that I never told the truth, or not the whole truth. What was the point of starting now?

"Hey," he said, his face filled with alarm. "What do you mean, you don't know?"He put his hand on my waist. "What's wrong?""

I stared at him, my mouth slightly agape, as I considered how to respond. Emotional alternatives appeared in front of me, like tiles on a color wheel. In one version, I was sad and defenseless, my face on his shoulder as I begged him to take me home. In another, I was charming and seductive, luring him into a nearby office to distract him with want, instilling us both with a primitive performance that I could physically enjoy but feared I'd never genuinely experience.

I considered general poverty when analyzing key affective reactions. Number 10 on Cleckley's list refers to the sociopath's incapacity to experience certain emotions. For the first time, I recognized the importance of its perfection. This was how I used to "choose" feelings. I had no conscience that drew me to any one tile. They were essentially options open to me. Like clothing taken from a stranger's wardrobe, they hang limp and lifeless, devoid of any natural spark. This was my emotional experience: a vivid smorgasbord of affective reactions, undoubtedly crafted over a lifetime of observation.

David furrowed his brow, indicating that I was taking too long to make a decision. Even more obvious was his denial. He'd succumbed to the same spell as everyone else who knew me, putting himself onto me rather than seeing me. David was, after all, a good person. He wanted me to be a nice person, too. But what have I done to nice people? I weakened them. I dyed them. I contaminated them. But I wasn't about to do that to him. Not anymore.

I forced a faint smile and chose a tile on the opposite end of David's spectrum, leaning aggressively toward indifference.

"Nothing's wrong," I replied abruptly, my voice calm. "I was trying to remember the merchandise count." I pointed to the merchandise counter, which was conveniently located in a corner of the room. "I always forget," I admitted nonchalantly.

David frowned. I could tell he wasn't convinced, so I added more dishonesty to soften the edges. "I apologize if I seem out of it. We just came here from Everly's, and I've been drinking all day." I smiled and shook my head, as if responding to an inside joke. I was now harming him by choosing phrases that would provoke the emotions he feared the most: exclusion. Confusion. Irrelevance.

He took a deep breath. "I thought you worked at the counseling center on Thursdays."

The message was absolutely clear. He told me he loved me. He was subtly letting me know that he had paid attention when I described my schedule over the phone. He was demonstrating how much he was prepared to attempt, even now, to accept me. But it was enough. And I didn't care.

I perceived unresponsiveness in general interpersonal relationships. The twelfth item on Cleckley's list refers to a sociopath's refusal to reciprocate affection or trust.

I rolled my eyes. "Yeah, no," I said, faking frustration. "I decided to skip work for the show," I lied simply. Then I fired another missile at his failing fortifications. "What are you doing here?"

The blood drained from his face, and I worried he'd crack. But he pressed on. "We talked about this weeks ago," he repeated. "This is Everly's last show. I understand it's a big thing. I wanted to be here. Y'know?" Then, gently, "for you."

I nodded carefully and pouted, feeling disappointed in myself. "Hmm. "I don't recall that." I shrugged. "But it's really sweet that you came."

Then I observed as he fought with how to deal with my deception, which was killing him much more slowly than I had imagined. I saw him flounder, but I did nothing to help.

I smiled as wide as I could and walked forward to embrace him. I was confident that this embarrassing public display of devotion would accomplish two things. It would authenticate my insincerity while erasing any sincerity that the first embrace had revealed. But when I felt his arms tighten around my waist, I was hit by a wave of grief. I rested my head on his shoulder and took long breaths. It felt great to be in his embrace. So honest. Very safe. "I love you," I muttered too softly for him to hear.

It was a peace I could never maintain but could sense when he held me. A future with David was my version of phantom limb syndrome—it was both real and unreal, which was frustrating. I wanted to stay there forever, floating in the calm. But I knew I couldn't.

Dorian's hillside pool floats on stilts above the Hollywood Hills, with the city spread out like a blanket of inverted stars beyond an infinity deck. I took a deep breath and jumped in, slicing through the water's surface before landing at the pool's bottom. God, I wanted to stay there.

I counted as high as I could before breaking through the surface and swimming to Everly, who was sitting on the edge of the adjoining Jacuzzi. She appeared sad.

"I can't believe you," she replied.

I gave her a disappointed pout. It was about three in the morning. Everly and I had driven up to her bandmate's house to commemorate the conclusion of their tenure. Initially, the atmosphere had been buoyant. Everly and her band were exuberant and jubilant after their performance. And I was content to coast on the wave of their feelings. But when their adrenaline subsided, so did my emotions. Shortly after we got into the pool for a moonlight swim, I noticed myself slipping back into a familiar sense of apathy. So I took advantage of the chance to pull off the bandage and tell Everly that I was going to quit.

"I knew you would be disappointed," I murmured, glancing up at my friend. "But I just can't do it anymore." I paused before adding, "I understand if you don't want to be friends."

Everly looked at me like I was insane. "What the fuck, Patric?" Do you think I wouldn't want to be friends anymore?"

She prodded me with her foot to capture my complete attention. "Be honest," she begged me. "Don't you feel the same way I do about you?" Don't you realize that more than anything else, you're my best friend, and I adore you?"

"It's not that I don't feel it," I explained. "I don't trust it. You don't understand—it's not only my view of love that is skewed. It belongs to other people as well." I shook my head.

"People never loved me, Everly. They enjoy the darkness in me. They witness the darkness, recklessness, and emotional liberation and are drawn to it. They want it for themselves. So they steal it. They utilize me for it. Steal my ego strength. Ride my wicked coattails. And I utilize them right back."

I tilted my head. "But, after a while, one of two things always occurs. Either I become irritated and cut off the supply, or their guilt sets in and I become the scapegoat." I glared, a slight fury churning at the back of my throat. I glared defiantly at her. "And you know what? "I am fucking over it."

"Over what?" she asked.

"I mean, I'm done being invisible," I said, my ire rising. "Seriously. Why should I be the one hiding under some fucking'mask of sanity'? "I am not the insane one," I said, pointing to the metropolis below. "Are those people out there? These are the insane ones. Those who deny their darkness. Those who act as if sociopathy is a horrible condition to which they cannot possibly connect. The ones talking shit about the word as if it weren't the name of the standoffish girl at school with whom they're all secretly trying to fuck. "Or imitate."

I hissed back at Everly. "I may be a sociopath, but I can accept that. What about those individuals out there?" I pointed again at the skyline. "They don't get to have an opinion about it. They cannot express their opinions on sadness, anxiety, or PTSD. Do you know why? I am not a fucking Rorschach. I'm not here to project their basic nonsense. I'm not a self-object for whatever insane version of love they've decided is the only one."

"But they're not all crazy, Patric," Everly insisted. "Believe it or not, there are individuals in the world who adore you. People like me. "People like David."

I lowered my gaze and studied this undeniable reality, briefly distracted by the moon's glittering reflection on the water's surface. "I know," I confessed. "And deep down in my heart, I know you love me. And I am sure David does, too." I shrugged helplessly. "But he doesn't accept me."

"You said Max accepted you, though," Everly pointed out. "And that didn't work out."

"Because he only accepted my darkness," I explained. I held out my hands. "It's like David was too far left and Max was too far right." I took a breath and responded, "I need to find the middle."

Everly looked perplexed. "And what is that?""

"I am." I became silent as the weight of my sentence sunk in. "I'm a sociopath," I explained. "I am right in the center of the spectrum. But I've spent my entire life using non-sociopaths as compasses." I shook my head. "First, I wanted to be good for my mom," I told her. "Then I wanted to be good to David. But that method repeatedly failed." I inhaled slowly. "The reality is that I need to want to do well for myself. I have to want to make good choices because I see the benefits, not because someone else is forcing me to."

I moved away from Everly and leaned my head against the pool's edge. I glanced at the massive concrete slab that framed one side of the home, recalling Rothko's expressionist color fields.

"It's exactly like you stated. I am one person with David. You're with a different person now. And unseen to almost everyone else. That must end. I need to accept myself all the time. I need to be myself all the time. That's the only way I'll ever be able to maintain my life." I stopped, then continued, "That's the only way I'll ever be able to share my life."

I looked down at the water again and thought how difficult it would be to entirely give up invisibility. That ultraviolet component of my personality has influenced my life in numerous ways. It has given me access to people, places, and adventures that most people would do everything to have.

A kaleidoscope of recollections raced across my head. The roughness of bricks in an underground passage, as seen from the balcony of an abandoned hotel. I smiled as I remembered running my fingers through Samson's fur, his head in my lap, as we spent a stolen day. Or the evenings I rushed through Laurel Canyon, feeling the reverb of Miles Davis' trumpet booming from rented speakers and rebounding off the rocks. I closed my eyes and urged myself to be grateful—for the fact that I was never upset by the vast expanse of isolation or the feel of a stranger's garment on my skin. To be sure, it was an exceptional life. Unconventional, but remarkable.

"When do you think you'll start?"" Everly inquired, playfully interrupting my daydream.

"Tomorrow," I answered. Then I sang along to Jane's Addiction's

"Gonna kick tomorrow!""

Everly laughed. "Well, I've got news for you, sweetheart," she told me. "It's already tomorrow."

I leaned defiantly over the edge of the pool, flashing a naughty grin. "Well, I guess I'd better get started."

Everly then laughed and shoved me backward, causing me to fall beneath the surface.

I was already underwater when I realized I'd forgotten to breathe. I realized this feeling had long since become my norm. The water flowed over my face and into my eyes, blocking my panoramic vision of the city. Under the surface, the false scene flashed once more against my eyelids. Its edges sparkled once more before gradually fading into the underwater blackness, *becoming nothing more than a memory.*

EPILOGUE

David's acceptance of my sociopathic symptoms—to see the little girl still fleeing, lost and lonely in the empty house of her own mind—changed my life. Without my convenient dose of behavioral prescriptions and psychological shortcuts, I was afraid I'd give in to apathy. My lack of emotion was like a pitch-black labyrinth of caves accessible only via a steep psychological drop—the emptiest location on the planet. But suddenly David's words echoed across the chamber. "It's just darkness," he'd explain. "You are currently unhappy with your apathy. You are fatigued and do not want to battle. It's okay. "Just relax and let it go."

David was the one who encouraged me to continue journaling and, eventually, writing. His belief in me helped me navigate the darkness. He encouraged me to believe in myself as a capable partner, wife, and mother.

Granted, my motherhood experience was not entirely traditional. It wasn't like anything I'd read about in novels or seen on television. When our son was born, I was not overwhelmed with emotion. I did not receive the powerful wave of "perfect" love that had been promised. And I was angry. Though I didn't realize it at the time, I'd been hoping (again) that I, too, would be overcome with emotion when I first saw my child. Throughout my pregnancy, I had secretly hoped that, unlike every other "important" life event, this most basic of human emotional sensations would not be taken away from me. So, when my baby was born, and I was once again unable to connect with my emotions, I was enraged.

"Do you want to hold him?" the delivery nurse said.

"No," I responded, furious at the stupidity of my optimism.

But David did. David removed his shirt moments after our kid was delivered, allowing our newborn to enjoy his first skin-to-skin contact. David was the one who taught him how to swaddle, gave him baths, took him on long walks, and did everything else during his first few weeks of paternity leave. And it was David who persuaded me that everything was not lost.

"Patric, none of this is easy," he explained as he prepared to return to work. "All the movies and books, none of it prepares you for this." He gestured around our bedroom, which had been converted into a makeshift nursery. "If anything, being a sociopath is probably beneficial right now. You're really calm and organized. "I'm so exhausted that I can't think straight." He gave a gentle grin to the young boy sleeping in my arms. "I know you love that baby," he continued. "Just because your love is different doesn't mean it doesn't count."

When David departed for work that day, I was honest with my infant son. "You are weird for a mom, babe," I told him. "So I can't promise your childhood is going to be entirely normal." I took a moment to acknowledge, "I also can't promise that the next time we go to the grocery store, if we see that doggie locked in the hot car again, I'm not going to break him out, then tell Daddy we got him at the shelter." I tenderly laid his toy turtle on his small chest, as if it were an oath. "But I can assure you that I will never put you in danger. You will never be safer than when you are with me, I promised. I'll never lie to you."

And I managed to uphold the commitment.

Made in the USA
Las Vegas, NV
19 September 2024

95506329R00085

Embracing The Sociopath Within

"Representation is important. I'm sharing my experience because it highlights a truth that no one wants to admit: darkness lurks in the most unexpected places. I'm a criminal with no prior record. I'm a master at disguise. I've never been caught. I've rarely been sorry. I'm friendly. I am responsible. I'm invisible. I mix well. I am a 21st-century psychopath. And I wrote this book because I realize I am not alone."

— Patric Gagne

ISBN 9798329588385

90000

9 798329 588385